Clojure Data Structures and Algorithms Cookbook

25 recipes to deeply understand and implement advanced algorithms in Clojure

Rafik Naccache

BIRMINGHAM - MUMBAI

Clojure Data Structures and Algorithms Cookbook

First published: August 2015

Production reference: 1140815

Published by Packt Publishing Ltd.
Livery Place
35 Livery Street
Birmingham B3 2PB, UK.

ISBN 978-1-78528-145-7

www.packtpub.com

Credits

Author

Rafik Naccache

Reviewers

Vitomir Kovanović

Muktabh Mayank

Commissioning Editor

Nadeem N. Bagban

Acquisition Editor

Tushar Gupta

Content Development Editor

Natasha DSouza

Technical Editor

Vivek Pala

Copy Editors

Brandt D'Mello

Neha Vyas

Project Coordinator

Vijay Kushlani

Proofreader

Safis Editing

Indexer

Mariammal Chettiyar

Production Coordinator

Conidon Miranda

Cover Work

Conidon Miranda

About the Author

Rafik Naccache is a Tunisian, who is experienced in software architecture and is an emergent technology enthusiast. He earned his bachelor's degree in computer science engineering from the University of Tunis in 2001. Rafik fell in love with Clojure back in 2012 and has been developing it professionally since 2013. He has occupied various positions in the telecom and banking sectors and has launched a few innovative start-ups on the Internet, in which he was able to deploy Clojure apps. He also founded the Tunisian Clojure enthusiasts community. He contributes to open source projects such as Cryogen (`https://github.com/cryogen-project/cryogen/graphs/contributors`) and Milestones (`https://github.com/automagictools/milestones`).

First of all, I am grateful to my mom, Safia, and dad, Abdelaziz, for the love and education that they generously provided me with. Thanks to Spectrum ZX, which we had back in the 80s. I grew as addicted to computers as I am right now, and this was the start of everything.

I would also like to thank my in-laws, aunt Zohra and uncle Hammadi, who always supported me and had blind and unconditional faith in the work I did. They really wanted to see this book published.

I am very thankful to my editors Tushar Gupta, Vivek Pala, and Natasha Dsouza; and reviewers, Vitomir Kovanovic and Multabh Mayank, for the valuable advice and professional guidance that they provided to accomplish this book.

I would especially like to thank my friends Anas Zdadou and Sahbi Chakroun and my family: Tselma, Soussou, Dah, Hafedh, Zazza, and Idriss. I owe so much to you all.

However, most of all, I am extremely grateful to my super wife, Khawla, who patiently had to suffer my absence while I wrote this book. During this period, she always kept her smile on and never complained. I can say that this book would probably never have been possible if she hadn't been there all along with our little Fatma Ezzahra, casting a light to help brighten my hard journey toward achievement and success.

About the Reviewers

Vitomir Kovanović is a PhD student at the School of Informatics in the University of Edinburgh, UK. He received an MSc degree in computer science and software engineering in 2011 and a BSc degree in information systems and business administration in 2009 from the University of Belgrade, Serbia. His research interests include learning analytics, educational data mining, and online education. He is a member of the Society for Learning Analytics Research and the program committees of several conferences and journals in technology-enhanced learning. In his PhD research, he focuses on the use of trace data for understanding the effects of technology on the quality of the social learning process and learning outcomes. To find out more about him, visit `http://vitomir.kovanovic.info/`.

www.PacktPub.com

Support files, eBooks, discount offers, and more

For support files and downloads related to your book, please visit www.PacktPub.com.

Did you know that Packt offers eBook versions of every book published, with PDF and ePub files available? You can upgrade to the eBook version at www.PacktPub.com and as a print book customer, you are entitled to a discount on the eBook copy. Get in touch with us at service@packtpub.com for more details.

At www.PacktPub.com, you can also read a collection of free technical articles, sign up for a range of free newsletters and receive exclusive discounts and offers on Packt books and eBooks.

https://www2.packtpub.com/books/subscription/packtlib

Do you need instant solutions to your IT questions? PacktLib is Packt's online digital book library. Here, you can search, access, and read Packt's entire library of books.

Why Subscribe?

- ▸ Fully searchable across every book published by Packt
- ▸ Copy and paste, print, and bookmark content
- ▸ On demand and accessible via a web browser

Free Access for Packt account holders

If you have an account with Packt at www.PacktPub.com, you can use this to access PacktLib today and view 9 entirely free books. Simply use your login credentials for immediate access.

Table of Contents

Preface

The invention of Lisp by John McCarthy in 1958 is certainly one of the most seminal events in the history of computer science. Originally intended as a way of porting Alonzo Church's lambda calculus theory into the realm of computer programs, Lisp pioneered many original ideas, such as higher order functions, recursion, and even garbage collection that proved to be so highly pragmatic that practically every modern high-level programming language of today is very likely built on some significant Lisp legacy.

However, beyond any practical or technical contribution, Lisp's most important trait is undeniably its unparalleled expressiveness. It's simplistic, yet its extremely elegant syntax propels it as a privileged tool for creative computer scientists, one which you could use as a powerful "building material" to erect algorithmic monuments without worrying about ancillary implementation details. It's certainly this ability of abstracting away "incidental complexity" that made Lisp the language for conducting Artificial Intelligence experiments, for instance.

Clojure, as a modern Lisp language, leverages this extraordinary expressive power to provide a platform that is highly suitable for algorithmic exploration. The abstractions it offers, the functional approach it suggests, as well as the built-in concurrency it supports, are all valuable facilities that enable straight and noise-free problem solving, which is an alternative way of approaching algorithms' design and sometimes, even innovative out-of-the-box thinking.

This book tries to underpin this idea. Using Clojure, we'll consider seven areas of algorithmic challenges and try to address them by taking advantage of all the power that we can get from this Lisp dialect. Besides, while choosing these seven problem domains, I tried to attain two main objectives. First, I wanted to tackle algorithms that have concrete real-world usage, and theory in the recipes will only be present to serve well-defined use cases in our everyday work with computers. Second, I tried to come up with material as varied as possible, so that the recipes cover a wide range of topics, from compressing files and building parsers to designing HTML5 interactive games and assembling type inferencers.

As far as the recipes' general layout is concerned, at the beginning, you will be given a thorough introduction to the intuition and the theory behind the algorithm being studied. Then, I will elaborate on every recipe's detail, making sure that I've explained every step and extensively commented the code. At the end of every recipe, you will see a sample usage of what has been implemented. This way, you will be guided through the whole process: the algorithm inception, its implementation, and its testing. In this process, I hope to have had mirrored the Clojure interactive workflow, in which the developer builds their program function by function, going back and forth to his/her REPL.

I really enjoyed the process of writing this book. I can, for sure, assert that the Clojure promise of high expressive power has been fulfilled for this particular project, as I came up with quite complex algorithmic implementations with reasonable effort while being really productive. My only wish is that you, by the end of this work, will be as convinced by Clojure and Lisp as I am.

You can reach me at @turbopape on Twitter, I'll answer, with extreme pleasure, all your questions.

What this book covers

Chapter 1, *Revisiting Arrays*, explores some interesting alternative uses for the array data structure. You'll learn in this recipe how to implement data compression using the LZ77 algorithm. Then, we'll see how you can use Pascal's triangle in order to draw some fractals. Next, we'll design a little multithreaded program execution simulator. We will end this chapter by studying an algorithm used to handle a call stack frames operation during a program execution.

Chapter 2, *Alternative Linked Lists*, delves into the advanced matters related to linked lists. We will cover a method using XOR addressing in order to get doubly linked lists. We'll then cover how to speed up a linked list's element retrieval, thanks to caching. We'll also use this data structure to build a shift-reduce parser. At the end, we'll explore an immutable functional data representation of linked lists by using the skew binary numbers representation.

Chapter 3, *Walking Down Forests of Data*, focuses on recipes related to tree data structure. First, we'll cover the self-balancing, search-optimized splay tree. Then, we'll elaborate on B-trees and show you how we can use a B-tree in order to build a key-value data store. Next, we'll show you how ropes can be used in order to create an undo-capable text editor. The last recipe of this chapter will be about tries and how they allow you to create efficient autocomplete engines.

Chapter 4, Making Decisions with the Help of Science, gives you an overview of a few machine learning and optimization algorithms. We'll first show you an approach that is used to build live recommendation engines. Then, we'll use the branch and bound algorithm to solve a cost/ profit optimization problem, which can only accept a natural numbers solution. Next, we'll use the Dijkstra algorithm in order to find the optimal paths in graphs. The final recipe in this chapter is about using the LexRank algorithm in order to summarize text documents.

Chapter 5, Programming with Logic, focuses on logic programming. We'll first use this highly declarative approach in order to draw interesting facts out of a social networking website's traffic data. Then, we'll show you how a simple type inferencer can be built using logic programming. At the end, we'll design a simple IA module capable of playing one round of checkers.

Chapter 6, Sharing by Communicating, gives particular attention to asynchronous programming. We'll begin by using this concurrency paradigm in order to build a tiny web scraper. Then, we'll go through the process of creating an interactive HTML5 game. Finally, we'll design an online taxi-booking platform as a complex system that could benefit from asynchronous programming.

Chapter 7, Transformations as First-class Citizens, dives into a few particular algorithmic cases inherent to the functional nature of Clojure. We'll start by designing a simple recursive descent parser, making use of the efficient mutual recursion offered by the Trampoline construct. Then, we'll see the new Clojure 1.7 feature—the transducers—in action while developing a mini firewall simulator. Finally, we'll introduce you to the continuation-passing style while designing a little symbolic expression unification engine.

What you need for this book

To be able to follow along, you need a running Clojure REPL. Getting to a working Clojure environment is generally done through Leiningen (`https://leiningen.org`), which will need a JVM installation in order to be able to work. Clojure 1.6 will be fine for all the recipes except for the second recipe in *Chapter 7, Transformations as First-class Citizens*, which will need Clojure 1.7. Though not absolutely necessary, you can consider using a full-fledged Clojure development environment, such as Emacs/CIDER, IntelliJ/Cursive, Light Table, or Nightcode.

Who this book is for

This book is for intermediate Clojure developers who can read and write in this language quite comfortably. Besides, it is assumed that you have some knowledge of how to set up Clojure projects, include dependencies, how to run REPLs, and so on through Leiningen and Figwheel. No prior awareness of any of the algorithms covered in this book is needed, and, when appropriate, pointers are given to the explanation material about any theory related to them.

Sections

In this book, you will find several headings that appear frequently (Getting ready, How to do it, How it works, There's more, and See also).

To give clear instructions on how to complete a recipe, we use these sections as follows:

Getting ready

This section tells you what to expect in the recipe, and describes how to set up any software or any preliminary settings required for the recipe.

How to do it...

This section contains the steps required to follow the recipe.

How it works...

This section usually consists of a detailed explanation of what happened in the previous section.

There's more...

This section consists of additional information about the recipe in order to make the reader more knowledgeable about the recipe.

See also

This section provides helpful links to other useful information for the recipe.

Conventions

In this book, you will find a number of styles of text that distinguish between different kinds of information. Here are some examples of these styles, and an explanation of their meaning.

Code words in text, database table names, folder names, filenames, file extensions, pathnames, dummy URLs, user input, and Twitter handles are shown as follows:
"We can use the `core.match` library in our program so we can use pattern matching."

A block of code is set as follows:

```
(defn accept-requests!
  [c->m
   requests]
  (go
    (while true
      (let [r (<! c->m)]
        ;;If something comes up
        ;;through the channel
        (swap! requests conj r)))))
```

Any command-line input or output is written as follows:

```
# lein repl
```

New terms and **important words** are shown in bold. Words that you see on the screen, in menus or dialog boxes for example, appear in the text like this: "This step is followed when **p** is not at the root and **p** and **x** are aligned to the left or right, as shown in the next figure."

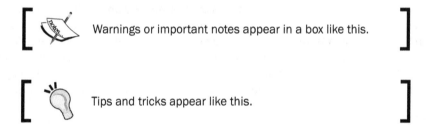

> Warnings or important notes appear in a box like this.

> Tips and tricks appear like this.

Reader feedback

Feedback from our readers is always welcome. Let us know what you think about this book—what you liked or may have disliked. Reader feedback is important for us to develop titles that you really get the most out of.

To send us general feedback, simply send an e-mail to feedback@packtpub.com, and mention the book title via the subject of your message.

If there is a topic that you have expertise in and you are interested in either writing or contributing to a book, see our author guide on www.packtpub.com/authors.

Customer support

Now that you are the proud owner of a Packt book, we have a number of things to help you to get the most from your purchase.

Downloading the example code

You can download the example code files for all Packt books you have purchased from your account at http://www.packtpub.com. If you purchased this book elsewhere, you can visit http://www.packtpub.com/support and register to have the files e-mailed directly to you.

Errata

Although we have taken every care to ensure the accuracy of our content, mistakes do happen. If you find a mistake in one of our books—maybe a mistake in the text or the code—we would be grateful if you would report this to us. By doing so, you can save other readers from frustration and help us improve subsequent versions of this book. If you find any errata, please report them by visiting http://www.packtpub.com/submit-errata, selecting your book, clicking on the **errata submission form** link, and entering the details of your errata. Once your errata are verified, your submission will be accepted and the errata will be uploaded on our website, or added to any list of existing errata, under the Errata section of that title. Any existing errata can be viewed by selecting your title from http://www.packtpub.com/support.

Piracy

Piracy of copyright material on the Internet is an ongoing problem across all media. At Packt, we take the protection of our copyright and licenses very seriously. If you come across any illegal copies of our works, in any form, on the Internet, please provide us with the location address or website name immediately so that we can pursue a remedy.

Please contact us at copyright@packtpub.com with a link to the suspected pirated material.

We appreciate your help in protecting our authors, and our ability to bring you valuable content.

Questions

You can contact us at questions@packtpub.com if you are having a problem with any aspect of the book, and we will do our best to address it.

1

Revisiting Arrays

In this chapter, we will see how you can use array abstractions in Clojure to cover the following topics:

- ▶ Efficiently compressing a byte array
- ▶ Using Pascal's triangle to draw fractals
- ▶ Simulating multithreading using time-sharing
- ▶ Simulating a call stack using arrays

Introduction

In this book, we will go on a journey through the broad land of algorithms and data structures, taking a ride on the comfortable vehicle that is Clojure programming language.

First, we will take a look at arrays, exploring their particular structures to tackle problems as interesting as compression, fractal drawing, multithreading, and call stacks.

Then we will elaborate on linked lists, transforming them in to doubly linked lists. We will do this to speed up access to their elements, build parsers, and devise fast random access.

The next step of our trip will concern trees of data. We'll show you how to implement self-balancing red-black trees, how to design efficient key-value stores — thanks to B-trees (way to go in order to design undo-capable text editors), and lastly, a methodology to construct autocomplete text typing systems.

After that, we'll focus on exploring some optimization and machine-learning techniques. We will see how to set up a recommendation engine, the way to go to optimize a problem where costs and profits are involved, a methodology to find the best possible paths in graphs, and how to summarize texts.

Then we'll study the topic of logic programming, analyzing some website traffic logs to detect visitors of interest to us. Doing this, we'll dive into the problem of type inferencing for the Java language, and simulate a turn of a checkers game.

At that point, we'll talk about asynchronous programming as a means of tackling difficult problems. We'll build a tiny web spider, design an interactive HTML5 game, and design a complex online taxi-booking solution.

The last rally point of this trip, but certainly not the least, is that we'll have a look at the higher order functions and transducers at the heart of Clojure. We'll design a recursive descent parser using a trampoline, build a reusable mini firewall thanks to transducers, and lastly, explore the continuation passing style as a tool to design a simple unification engine.

This will be quite a tour, in which we will bring to life various real-world use cases related to the essential theory of computing as far as data structures and algorithms are involved, which are all served by the high expressive power of Clojure. By the end of this book, you'll be familiar with many of the advanced concepts that fuel most of the nontrivial applications of our world while you enhance your mastery of Clojure!

Efficiently compressing a byte array

Compressing a byte array is a matter of recognizing repeating patterns within a byte sequence and devising a method that can represent the same underlying information to take advantage of these discovered repetitions.

To get a rough idea of how this works, imagine having a sequence as:

```
["a" "a" "a" "b" "b" "b" "b" "b" "b" "b" "c" "c"]
```

It is intuitively more efficient to represent this as:

```
[3 times "a", 7 times "b", 2 times "c"]
```

Now, we are going to use a methodology based on a well-known algorithm, that is, the LZ77 compression method. LZ77 is, despite being quite old, the basis of most of all the well-known and currently used compression methods, especially the Deflate algorithm.

 Deflate is at the heart of the ZIP family of compression algorithms. It uses a slightly modified version of LZ77 plus a special encoding, that is, the Huffman encoding.

The point of LZ77 is to walk a sequence and recognize a pattern in the past elements that will occur in the upcoming elements, replacing those with a couple of values: how many elements should go backwards in order to locate the recurring pattern, which is called "distance"; and how long is the recurring pattern, which is labeled as "length".

The iteration of the LZ77 compression would look as follows:

1. At any point of time, the algorithm is processing a particular element, which is located at the current position. Consider a window of the size *n,* as a set of *n* elements preceding the one that is occupying current position, and consider lookahead as the rest of the elements up until the input's end.

2. Begin with the first element of the input.

3. Move on to the next element.

4. Find in the window (that is, past *n* elements), the longest pattern that can be found in lookahead.

5. If such a sequence is found, consider distance as the location where, the matching sequence was found, expressed in regards to the current position, consider length as the length of the matching pattern, and proceed with the two following actions:

   ❑ Replace the match in lookahead by "distance" and "length".

   ❑ Move forward using the "length" elements and resume algorithm execution at step 4.

6. Otherwise, resume at step 3.

The procedure to uncompress is as follows:

1. Walk the compressed sequence.

2. If the "distance" and "length" are found, go back to the "distance" elements and replace this couple with the "length" elements.

3. If not, lay out the element that you've found.

Let's see this in action in Clojure!

How to do it...

1. First of all, here is the ns declaration containing the Clojure facilities that we are going to use:

   ```
   (ns recipe1.core
    (:require [clojure.set :as cset]))
    ;; => we'll need set operations later on.
   ```

2. Let's begin by working on the uncompressing part. First of all, we need an expand function that takes the source array as a vector of the elements distance and length and generates a repetition of a sub-vector of the last distance characters from the source array until the length is reached:

   ```
   (defn expand
    [the-vector
     distance
   ```

```
                      length]
        (let [end (count the-vector)
                start (- end
                           distance)
;;=> Here we go backwards 'distance' elements.
                pattern (subvec the-vector
                                   start
                                   end)]        ;=> We have our pattern.
            (into [] (take length     ;=> We exactly take "length" from
                      (cycle pattern)))))
;; an infinite repetition of our pattern.
```

3. Now, let's define `un-LZ77` using `expand` function while walking through a sequence of bytes:

```
(defn un-LZ77
   [bytes]
   (loop [result []
            remaining bytes]
;;=> We recur over the contents of the array.
      (if (seq remaining)
         (let [current (first remaining)
                 the-rest (rest remaining)]
;=> Current element under scrutiny;
            (if-not (vector? Current)
;=> If it is not a vector, add to result
               (recur (conj result
;;       the very element, and move on.
                               current)
                     the-rest)
               (recur (into result (expand result
;;=> This is a vector, then we'll expand here and move on
                                            (current 0)
                                            (current 1)))
                     the-rest)))
         result)))
;;=> end of recursion, return result.
```

4. Now let's address the topic of compressing. First of all, we need to grab all sub-vectors, as we'll have to find matches between window and lookahead and then pick the longest one among them:

```
(defn all-subvecs-from-beginning

;;=> this function will generate a set of all sub-vectors starting
;; from begin

  [v]

  (set (map #(subvec v 0 %)

;;=> we apply subvec from 0 to all indices from 1 up to the size
;; of the array + 1.

            (range 1 (inc (count v)))))))


(defn all-subvecs

;;=> this function will generate all

  [v]           ;          sub-vectors, applying

  (loop [result #{}

;;        all-subvecs from beginning to

;;        all possible beginnings.

         remaining v]

    (if (seq remaining)

      (recur (into result

                   (all-subvecs-from-beginning remaining))

             (into[]  (rest remaining)))

;;=> We recur fetching all sub-vectors for next beginning.


      result)))

;;=> end of recursion, I return result.
```

5. Now we define a function to grab the longest match in `left array` with the beginning of `right array`:

```
(defn longest-match-w-beginning

  [left-array right-array]

  (let [all-left-chunks (all-subvecs left-array)

                              all-right-chunks-from-beginning

;;=> I take all sub-vectors from left-array

        (all-subvecs-from-beginning right-array)

;;=> I take all sub-vectors from right-array
```

```
     all-matches (cset/intersection all-right-chunks-from-beginning
                                    all-left-chunks)]
;;=> I get all the matchings using intersection on sets
     (->> all-matches
          (sort-by count >)
          first)))
;=> Then I return the longest match, sorting them
;; by decreasing order and taking the first element.
```

6. With the longest match function in hand, we need a function to tell us where where is this match exactly located   inside the window:

```
(defn pos-of-subvec
  [sv v]
  {:pre [(<= (count sv)
             (count v))]}
;;=> I verify that sv elements are less than v's.
  (loop
      [cursor 0]
    (if (or (empty? v)
;;=> If on of the vectors is empty
            (empty? sv)
            (= cursor   (count v)))
;; or the cursor ended-up exiting v,
      nil                ;; we return nil
      (if (= (subvec v cursor
;; => If we found that the v sub-vector
                     (+ (count sv)
;;    beginning with cursor up to sv count
                        cursor)) sv)
;; is equal to sv cursor
;; we return cursor, this is where the match is.
        (recur (inc cursor)))))))
;=> We recur incrementing the cursor
```

7. Armed with the toolbox we've built so far, let's devise an LZ77 step:

```
(defn LZ77-STEP
  [window look-ahead]
  (let [longest (longest-match-w-beginning window
  look-ahead)]              ;;=> We find the Longest match,
    (if-let [pos-subv-w (pos-of-subvec longest window)]
;;=> If there is a match  we find its position in window.
      (let [distance (-  (count window) pos-subv-w)
;;=> the distance,
            pos-subv-l (pos-of-subvec longest
                                         look-ahead)
;;=> the position of the match in look-ahead
            the-char (first (subvec look-ahead
                                      (+ pos-subv-l
                                         (count longest))))]
;;=> the first element occuring after the match
        {:distance distance
         :length (count longest)
         :char the-char})
;;=> and we return information about match
        {:distance 0
         :length 0
         :char (first look-ahead)}))))
;;=> We did not find a match, we emit zeros  for "distance"
;; and "length", and first element of lookahead as first char
;; occurring after the (non-)match.
```

8. Finally, we will write the main LZ77 compression function as follows:

```
(defn LZ77
[bytes-array
 window-size]
(->> (loop [result []
            cursor 0
            window []
```

```
                  look-ahead bytes-array]
;;=> we begin with position 0; and everything as look-ahead.
         (if (empty? look-ahead)
           result
;;=> end of recursion, I emit result.
            (let [this-step-output (LZ77-STEP window look-ahead)
                  distance (:distance this-step-output)
                  length (:length this-step-output)
                  literal (:char this-step-output)
;;=> We grab informations about this step output
                  raw-new-cursor (+ cursor

                                    length

                                    1)
                  new-cursor (min raw-new-cursor

                                  (count bytes-array))
;;=> We compute the new-cursor, that is, where to go in the next
;; step
;;which is capped by count of bytes-array
                  new-window (subvec bytes-array

                                     (max 0 (inc (- new-cursor

                                                    window-size)))

                                     new-cursor)
;;=> new window is window-size elements back from new cursor.
                  new-look-ahead (subvec bytes-array

                                         new-cursor )]
;;=> new look-ahead is everything from new cursor on.
            (recur (conj result

                         [distance length]

                         literal)

                   new-cursor

                   new-window

                   new-look-ahead))))
;; and we recur with the new elements.
      (filter   (partial

                 not=
```

```
                    [0 0])))
;;=> We eliminate the entries related to non-matches
        (filter (comp
                not
                nil?))    ;;=> and any nils
        (into []))))       ;;=> and make a vector out of the output.
```

That's it! Now, let's see our code in action. Input into your REPL as follows:

```
(LZ77 ["a" "b" "c" "f" "a" "b" "c" "d"] 5)
;; => ["a" "b" "c" "f" [4 3] "d"]
(un-LZ77 ["a" "b" "c" "f" [4 3] "d"])
;; => ["a" "b" "c" "f" "a" "b" "c" "d"]
```

Using Pascal's triangle to draw fractals

Triangles are a particular matrix type. Each line contains exactly as many nonzero elements as the line index in the matrix. Here is a sample triangle depicted as a vector of vectors in Clojure:

```
[[1 0 0 0 0 0 0]
 [1 1 0 0 0 0 0]
 [1 1 1 0 0 0 0]
 [1 1 1 1 0 0 0]
 [1 1 1 1 1 0 0]
 [1 1 1 1 1 1 0]
 [1 1 1 1 1 1 1]]
```

Now, we can simply omit the zeros altogether and get a real triangle, graphically speaking:

```
[[1]
 [1 1]
 [1 1 1]
 [1 1 1 1]
 [1 1 1 1 1]
 [1 1 1 1 1 1]
 [1 1 1 1 1 1 1]
 [1 1 1 1 1 1 1 1 1]]
```

Pascal's triangle is a matrix whose elements are computed as the sum of the elements that are directly above it and the element to the left of the elements that are directly above it. The very first element is 1. This matrix was devised by Pascal as a means of computing the powers of binomials. Here's a Pascal's triangle for up to seven lines:

```
[[1]
 [1 1]
 [1 2 1]
 [1 3 3 1]
 [1 4 6 4 1]
 [1 5 10 10 5 1]
 [1 6 15 20 15 6 1]]
```

If we look at this Pascal's triangle, then a binomial, let's say *(a+b)*, elevated to the power 4 is computed by extracting the coefficient from the row with index 4 (first row is having index 0. The resulting polynomial is: *a4b+4a3b+6a2b2+4ab3+ab4*.

Now, it happens that plotting odd elements from a Pascal's triangle yields a fractal, that is, an image that infinitely repeats itself.

 Such a fractal derived from plotting the odd elements of a Pascal's triangle is known as the Sierpinski triangle.

If you closely watch the triangle's structure, you'll notice that each line is symmetrical. As such, for the sake of efficiency, you only have to compute half of a line at a time and append it to its own mirrored copy to get the whole line.

Besides, as our main purpose is to draw fractals, we'll have to generate a huge Pascal's triangle, in order to have a proper image. Doing so will make us soon hit number limitations and we'll have to circumvent this. Luckily, summing the remainder of a division of two by two numbers leads to the same even properties, as if you've summed those very numbers. Then, our implementation will rely on this to come up with sufficiently big images; we'll create Pascal's triangles with the sums of the remainder of the division by two.

How to do it...

1. First of all we'll need to import, along with our `ns` declaration, some Java facilities to help us build the fractal and write it to a file:

```
(ns recipe2.core
  (:import (java.awt image.BufferedImage Color)
;=> so we can plot.
          (javax.imageio ImageIO)
          (java.io File)))      ;=> so we can write to a file.
```

2. Let's write a function to compute a particular row in a Pascal's triangle, As we've discussed, in a Pascal's triangle you compute a row of a particular index based on the one located directly above it (of the preceding index), that's why this function takes one row as input. Here we pass a `yield` function, permitting it to compute an element out of its immediately preceding neighbor and the element to the left of the preceding neighbor. Each time, we compute half a line and append it to its reverse:

```
(defn pascal-row-step
  [yield pascal-row]
;=> pascal-row is the one above the row we're computing
  {:pre [(> (get  pascal-row 0) 0)]}   ;=> We can only start from
[1]!
  (let [cnt-elts (count pascal-row)
        half-row (subvec pascal-row 0
                          (inc (double (/ cnt-elts 2))))
;;=> We compute half the above row
        padded-half-row (into [0] half-row)
;;=> and add a 0 to the beginning, as we'll use it in computation
        half-step (vec  (map (comp (partial apply yield)
                                  vec)
                        (partition 2 1
                                  padded-half-row)))
;;=> we compute the first half, summing the above element
;;        and the element at the left of the above one.
        other-half-step (vec  (if (even? cnt-elts)
                                (-> half-step
                                    butlast
                                    reverse)
                                (-> half-step
                                    reverse)))]
;;=> the mirror of the half we computed. If count elements is
;; even, we omit the last element from half-step.
    (into half-step other-half-step)))
;;=> we return half to which we append the mirror copy.
```

3. Now, we'll build the whole Pascal's triangle parameterized with the `yield` function:

```
(defn pascal-rows
  [yield row-number]
  (loop [nb 0
         result []
         latest-result [1]]
;=> We'll loop using pascal-row-step,
;;=> keeping track of the last
;;computed line at each step of the recursion.
```

```
        (if (<= nb row-number)
;;=> the counter did not still reach the end
        (recur (inc nb)
               (conj result latest-result)
               (pascal-row-step yield latest-result))
;;=> We recur incrementing the counter, feeding the new line to
;; result and keeping track of the last computed line.
        result)))

;;=> end of the recursion, emitting result.
```

4. We will also prepare a `yield` function to compute the remainder of the sum of two numbers:

```
(defn even-odd-yield
  [n1 n2]
  (mod (+ n1 n2) 2))
```

5. We will prepare a helper function to generate the fractals:

```
(def gr-triangles (partial pascal-rows even-odd-yield))
```

6. Now we can just launch the following to have our graphical 0-1 fractal representation:

```
(gr-triangles 10)
```

7. With `gr-triangles` under our belt, we have to plot points at the positions that hold 1. For this, we'll consider the cords of such positions to be the index of line and the index of elements in the vector held by this line that have the value 1:

```
(defn draw [size]
  (let [img (BufferedImage. size size BufferedImage/TYPE_INT_ARGB)
;;=> Creating img as a Buffered Image
        plot-rows (gr-triangles size)
;;=> computing the triangle of 0 and 1
        plots (for [x (range 0 size)
                    y (range 0 x)]
                (if (= 1 (get
                           (get plot-rows x) y))
                  [x y]))
;;=> we save the positions holding 1 in vectors. As the structure
;; is triangular;
;; the first counter, "x" goes up to "size", and the second one,
;; "y",
;;    goes up to "x"
```

```
        gfx (.getGraphics img)]
;;=> we get the graphics component, where to draw from the Java
;; Object.
    (.setColor gfx Color/WHITE)
    (.fillRect gfx 0 0 size size )
;;=> we set a white background for the image.
    (.setColor gfx Color/BLACK)
;;=> We set the pen color to black again
    (doseq [p (filter (comp not nil?)  plots)]
      (.drawLine gfx
            (get p 0)
              (get p 1)
              (get p 0)
              (get p 1)))
;;=> We plot, by drawing a line from and to the same point.
 (ImageIO/write img "png"
                  (File. "/your/location/result.png"))))
;;=> and we save the image as a png in this location.
;; Be sure to set a correct one when running on your machine !
```

Here is a zoomed-out image generated by this function of the size 10,000:

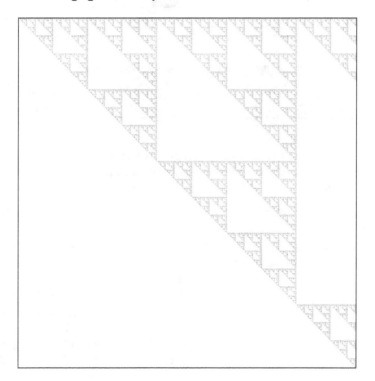

Here is a zoomed-in view of some parts of it:

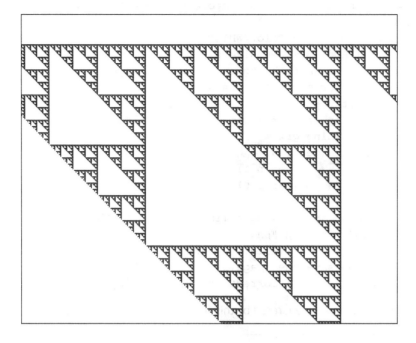

Here, the same triangles appear over and over again as you zoom in on the image.

Simulating multithreading using time-sharing

Time-sharing is about sharing a computing facility between multiple concurrent processes. At its very basic version, a scheduler decides , which one of these competing processes to execute at every single quantum of time. This way, even a single processor core, only capable of sequential operation, is able to spawn multiple threads, as if they were being executed in parallel.

One method of preventing race conditions, that is, multiple processes concurrently reading and writing wrong versions of the same shared place in memory, is locking. Imagine, for example, that there are two processes incrementing the same shared counter. Process 1 takes the value of the counter and overwrites it with the value + 1. If, meanwhile, process 2 does the same thing – that is, it reads the same version of the counter that process 1 reads for the very first time and overwrites it with the same value + 1 – you'd end up with the counter that will only be incremented once. Hence, locking this portion of code makes process 2 wait for process 1 until it finishes reading and writing, and only when process 1 is done and sets the lock free, process 2 will be allowed to play its part, leading to the correct final value of the counter + 2.

Managing locks can be too tedious. That's why it is often better to use high-level concurrency alternatives, such as those provided by Clojure: the software transactional memory (refs and atoms), agents, and core.async.

How to do it...

1. First of all, we'll begin importing some libraries that we will use:

```
(ns recipe3.core
  (:require [instaparse.core :as insta])
;;=> For parsing the code of our
              ;processes
  (:require [clojure.zip :as z])
;;=> To walk the parse-trees and generate processes instructions.
  (:require [clojure.pprint :refer :all]))
;;=> an Alias to easily pretty print our outputs.
```

 Instaparse (`https://github.com/engelberg/instaparse`) is a parser generator written in Clojure. To explain all of the mechanism behind Instaparse is beyond the scope of this book, but you should know that it handles **context-free grammar** (**CFG**) and generates parse trees of your input programs according to these grammar concepts.

2. To be able to pretty-print our output in the REPL, let's define an alias for `clojure.pprint/pprint`, so that we can make it more conveniently:

```
(def p pprint)
```

3. As we'll be spawning processes with instructions of their own, let's define a minimal language that `instaparse` will be able to interpret for us. Our language instructions for a single process are as follows:

```
heavy-op op1;
light-op op2;
lock l1;
medium-op op3;
unlock l1;
```

4. The previous snippet is self-explanatory. Our language only contains three types of operations: `heavy-op`, which are sorted according to the effort they need in order to be fully processed by the scheduler: `heavy-op`, `medium-op`, and finally `light-op`. Besides, we are able to lock and unlock a portion of our programs with the `lock` and `unlock` instructions. Each one of these instructions needs you to specify an identifier, so that they can be recognized in the scheduler output.

5. The grammar for such a language is:

```
(def r3-language
"S = INSTRS
  INSTRS = ((INSTR | LOCKED-INSTRS) <optional-whitespace>)*
  INSTR = HEAVY-OP | MEDIUM-OP | LIGHT-OP
  HEAVY-OP = <optional-whitespace> 'heavy-op' <whitespace> ID
<SEP>
  MEDIUM-OP = <optional-whitespace> 'medium-op' <whitespace> ID
<SEP>
  LIGHT-OP = <optional-whitespace> 'light-op' <whitespace> ID
<SEP>

  LOCKED-INSTRS = LOCK INSTRS UNLOCK
  LOCK = <optional-whitespace> 'lock' <whitespace> ID <SEP>
  UNLOCK = <optional-whitespace> 'unlock' <whitespace> ID <SEP>

  ID = #'[a-zA-Z0-9]+'
  PRIORITY = #'[0-9]+'

  whitespace = #'\\s+'
  optional-whitespace = #'\\s*'
  SEP = #'\\s*' ';'")
```

6. Note that identifiers between angle brackets will not be seen in the parse tree, so there's no use referring to the `white-space` tags, for instance.

7. Let's see what would be the Instaparse output for the program we wrote in the preceding code. For this, just type the following in your REPL:

```
(p  (insta/parse (insta/parser r3-language)
"heavy-op op1;
light-op op2;
lock l1;
medium-op op3;
unlock l1;"))
And you'll get :
[:S
  [:INSTRS
    [:INSTR [:HEAVY-OP "heavy-op" [:ID "op1"]]]
    [:INSTR [:LIGHT-OP "light-op" [:ID "op2"]]]
```

```
[:LOCKED-INSTRS
 [:LOCK "lock" [:ID "l1"]]
 [:INSTRS [:INSTR [:MEDIUM-OP "medium-op" [:ID "op3"]]]]
 [:UNLOCK "unlock" [:ID "l1"]]]]]]
```

8. We need to transform these nested vectors in to instructions. First of all, we will make use of the very handy instaparse function `transform` to eliminate the rules tags and get a more useful representation of our instructions. `transform` function takes a tag and applies a function to the elements next to it in the vector that this tag refers to:

```
(defn gen-program
  [parser program]
  (insta/transform
   {:S identity
    :INSTRS (fn [& args] (vec args))
    :INSTR identity
    :HEAVY-OP (fn [x y] {:inst-type :heavy-op :inst-id (get y 1)})
    :MEDIUM-OP (fn [x y] {:inst-type :medium-op :inst-id (get y
1)})
    :LIGHT-OP (fn [x y] {:inst-type :light-op :inst-id (get y 1)})
    :LOCKED-INSTRS (fn [& args] (vec args))
    :LOCK (fn [x y] {:inst-type :lock :inst-id {:lock (get y 1)}
})
    :UNLOCK (fn [x y] {:inst-type :unlock :inst-id {:unlock (get
y 1)}})}
;;=> This map tells 'transform' how to transform elements next to
;; each tag.
    (parser program)))

;; The raw parse tree emitted by Insaparse.
```

9. Here is the output of `gen-program`. Input the following code in the REPL:

```
(p (gen-program (insta/parser r3-language)
                    "heavy-op op1;
          light-op op2;
          lock l1;
          medium-op op3;
          unlock l1;"))
```

10. You'll get the following output:

```
[{:inst-type :heavy-op, :inst-id "op1"}
 {:inst-type :light-op, :inst-id "op2"}
 [{:inst-type :lock, :inst-id {:lock "l1"}}
  [{:inst-type :medium-op, :inst-id "op3"}
   {:inst-type :unlock, :inst-id {:unlock "l1"}}]]]
```

11. To get rid of the nesting that we still see here, we are going to use a zipper, which is a Clojure facility to walk trees. Basically, we will loop all the nested vector elements and only take maps, so that we end up with a nice, flat program structure. As this will be our actual process, we'll also append a `process-id` attribute and a `priority` attribute to its output:

```
(defn fire-a-process
  [grammar
   program
   process-id
   priority]
  (let [prsr (insta/parser grammar)        ;;=> the parser
        vec-instructions (gen-program prsr program)
;;=> the nested structure
        zpr (z/vector-zip vec-instructions)]
    (loop [result []
           loc (->  zpr z/down)]
      (if (z/end? loc)
;;=> the end of recursion, no more nodes to visit
        {:process-id process-id
         :instructions result
         :priority priority}          ;;=> We generate the process
        (recur (if (map? (z/node loc))
;;=> We only append to result the elements of type 'map'
                 (conj result (z/node loc))
                 result)
;;=> else we pass result as is in the recursion
               (z/next loc))))))
;=> and we recur with the next element.
```

12. Here is a process spawned by our program named `:process-1` that has the priority `10`. Input the following in your REPL:

```
(fire-a-process r3-language
                           "heavy-op op1;
           light-op op2;
           lock l1;
           medium-op op3;
           unlock l1;"
                           :process-1
                           10)
```

13. You'll get the following output:

```
{:process-id :process-1,
 :instructions
 [{:inst-type :heavy-op, :inst-id "op1"}
  {:inst-type :light-op, :inst-id "op2"}
  {:inst-type :lock, :inst-id {:lock "l1"}}
;;=> note that ':inst-id' of locks are {':lock' or ':unlock' id},
;; so a locking and an un-locking instructions are not mistaken
;; one for another.
  {:inst-type :medium-op, :inst-id "op3"}
  {:inst-type :unlock, :inst-id {:unlock "l1"}}],
 :priority 10}
```

14. Now, we need to set effort for each of our instructions, that is, how many processor cycles each one of them takes to be executed:

```
(def insts-effort {:heavy-op 10 :medium-op 5 :light-op 2 :lock 1
:unlock 1})
```

15. Now we'll concern ourselves with locking. First of all, we need to find the indices of locking instructions in our instructions vector:

```
(defn all-locks-indices   [instructions]
;;=> 'instructions' is the ':instructions vector' of the output of
;; fire-process.

  (let [locks (filter #(= (:inst-type %) :lock)
                       instructions)
;;=> We find out all the 'locks' in 'instructions'.
        lock-indices (map (fn [l] {:lock-id (l :inst-id)
                                   :lock-idx (.indexOf
instructions l)})
                          locks)]
;; And for every lock we find out its index in 'instructions,
;; and prepare a map with it.
    lock-indices))
;;=> output of this is : ({:lock-id {:lock "l1"}, :lock-idx 2})
```

16. With our locks recognized, we can tell which lock every instruction depends on. This is basically done by finding out which locks have indices inferior to the instruction index:

```
(defn the-locks-inst-depends-on
  [instructions instruction]
  (let [the-inst-idx (.indexOf instructions instruction)
        the-lock-idxs (all-locks-indices instructions)]
    (into []   (->> the-lock-idxs
                    (filter #(> the-inst-idx (:lock-idx %) ))
                    (map :lock-id)))))
```

17. We'll need a map that maintains the state of locks so the scheduler can track the locking and unlocking activities during the program execution with. We'll define `lock` and `un-lock` functions to do this:

```
(defn lock
  "locks lock lock-id in locks map"
  [locks process-id lock-id]
  (assoc locks lock-id {:locker process-id :locked true}))
(defn unlock
  "unlocks lock lock-id in locks map"
  [locks process-id lock-id]
  (assoc locks lock-id {:locker process-id :locked false}))
;;=> The locks state contains its locked state and which process
;; did lock it.
```

18. The locker process information, manipulated in the previous step is important. As some process' instruction can only be denied access to a shared resource by locks set by other processes contains, we need to track which is locking what. The `is-locked?` function relies on this mechanism to inform whether an instruction is locked at any point in time, so it cannot be fired by the scheduler:

```
(defn is-locked?
  [process-id
   instructions
   locks
   instruction]
  (let [inst-locks (the-locks-inst-depends-on instructions
instruction)]
    (some true? (map #(and (not= process-id ((get locks %)
:locker))
                           ((get locks %) :locked))
                inst-locks))))
;;=> If some of the locks the instruction depend on are locked
(:locked true)
;; and the locker is not its process, then it is considered as
;; locked.
```

19. Let's focus on the scheduler now. Imagine that some parts of a process have already been assigned some quanta of time. We need a map to maintain a state for all the processes regarding the parts that already have been processed so far. We'll call this map `scheduled`. Let's say that this map should look like the following:

```
[{:process-id :process-1
  :instructions
  [{:times [1 2 3], :inst-id "op1", :inst-type :heavy-op}
```

```
          {:times [4 5 6], :inst-id "op2", :inst-type :medium-op}]}
 {:process-id :process-id :process-2
  :instructions
  [{:times [7 8], :inst-id "op1", :inst-type :heavy-op}
   {:times [9 10], :inst-id "op2", :inst-type :medium-op}]}]
;;=> ':times' contain vectors of the time quantums allocated to
;; the instruction.
```

20. We'll prepare a helper function, `scheduled-processes-parts`, that'll count the number of quanta already allocated, and this will be handy in knowing whether an instruction is complete:

```
(defn scheduled-processes-parts
  [scheduled]
  (into [] (map  (fn [p] {:process-id (:process-id p)
                          :instructions (into []
(map (fn [i] {:inst-id (:inst-id i)
:inst-type (:inst-type i)
:count (count (:times i))})
(:instructions   p)))})
                scheduled)))
;;=> this functions just adds :count n to the map maintained in
;;"scheduled"
```

21. We'll use this function to implement `incomplete-instruction?`, `incomplete-process?`, and `more-incomplete-processes?` that we'll use later on:

```
(defn incomplete-instruction?
  [instruction-w-count]
(let [instr-effort (insts-effort (instruction-w-count :inst-type))
      instr-count (instruction-w-count :count)]
   (< instr-count instr-effort)))
(defn incomplete-process?
  [process-w-counts]
  (let [instrs-w-count (process-w-counts :instructions)]
    (some true? (map incomplete-instruction?
                     instrs-w-count))))
(defn more-incomplete-processes?
  [processes-w-count]
  (some true? (map incomplete-process?
                   processes-w-count)))
;=> processes-w-count is just another name for the "scheduled"
;;  state map.
```

22. Diving deeper into the implementation, let's now look at a single process and define a function that finds which instruction is to be fired if the scheduler decides to allocate a quantum to it. This translates to the first incomplete instruction if it is non-locked, that is, none of its locks have been set to `locked` by another process:

```
(defn find-inst-to-be-fired-in-process
  [locks
   process-id
   the-process-instructions
   the-process-scheduled-parts]
    (let [p-not-locked-instrs (set (->> the-process-instructions
(filter #(not (is-locked? process-id

the-process-instructions
locks
%)))))
;;=> A set of not locked instructions
p-incomplete-instrs (set (->> (:instructions  the-process-
scheduled-parts)
(filter incomplete-instruction?)
                                    (map #(dissoc % :count))))
;;=> A set of incomplete instructions
fireable-instrs (clojure.set/intersection p-not-locked-instrs
p-incomplete-instrs)
;;=> Their intersection
        instr-id-to-fire (->> fireable-instrs
(sort-by #(.indexOf the-process-instructions %) < )
                              (first)
                          (:inst-id))]
;;=> The first on of them
        instr-id-to-fire))
```

23. Now, let's write `progress-on-process!`, which considers one particular process, fires its fireable instruction — as found by the preceding function, and updates all `locks` and `scheduled` states. This is quite a long function, as it is the heart of the scheduler:

```
(defn progress-on-process!
  [locks-ref
   scheduled-ref
   the-process
   quantum]
    (let [the-process-instrs (the-process :instructions)
        processes-scheduled-parts (scheduled-processes-parts @
scheduled-ref)
```

```
                the-process-scheduled-parts (->> processes-scheduled-parts
(filter #(= (:process-id %)
(:process-id the-process)))
                                                        (first))]
```
;;=> Here we prepare the processes scheduled parts and take only
  ;; the relevant to the particular 'process-id'.
```
    (if-let [the-instr-to-fire-id (find-inst-to-be-fired-in-
process @locks-ref
(:process-id the-process)
the-process-instrs
the-process-scheduled-parts )]
```
;;=> If there is one instruction in "process-id" to be fired;
```
      (dosync
```
;;=> We use the refs, because we need to do transactions involving
  ;; both "scheduled" and "locks"
```
        (let [the-instr-to-fire (->> the-process-instrs
                                    (filter #(= (:inst-id %)
the-instr-to-fire-id))
                                                    (first))]
```
;;=> We get the entry relevant to this instruction-id
```
          (cond
          (= (:inst-type the-instr-to-fire) :lock ) (alter locks-ref
                                            lock
(:process-id the-process)
the-instr-to-fire-id)
            (= (:inst-type the-instr-to-fire) :unlock ) (alter
locks-ref
                                                    unlock
(:process-id the-process)
                                                        {:lock
(:unlock the-instr-to-fire-id)}))))
```
;;=> If it is a "lock" or "unlock", We update the "locks" state
;;   map
```
        (let [p-in-scheduled (->> @scheduled-ref
                                (filter #(= (:process-id %)
(:process-id the-process)))
                                                    (first))
```
   ;;=> To update the "scheduled" ref, we begin by finding the
    ;; ':process-d' in the processes vector
```
              instr-in-p-in-scheduled (->> (get p-in-scheduled
:instructions)
                                            (filter #(= (:inst-id %)
the-instr-to-fire-id))
                                                    (first))
```

```
            ;; Then We find the instruction in this process
                idx-p-in-scheduled (max 0 (.indexOf @scheduled-ref
p-in-scheduled))
                idx-inst-in-p-in-scheduled (max 0
(.indexOf (get p-in-scheduled :instructions)
instr-in-p-in-scheduled))
;;=> We compute the index of the instruction; or we set it at 0
  ;; if it is not found, which means it is the first time it is
  ;; scheduled.
                times-in-inst-in-p-in-scheduled (get
                                        (get (p-in-scheduled
:instructions)

idx-inst-in-p-in-scheduled) :times )
;;=> We get the times vector in "scheduled" related to this
            ;; instruction
                _ (alter scheduled-ref assoc-in [idx-p-in-scheduled
:instructions idx-inst-in-p-in-scheduled :times]
                    (conj times-in-inst-in-p-in-scheduled
quantum))])
;;=> And using assoc-in, with indices and keys as a "path
;;    vector", we Update the "scheduled" ref with times vector
;;    to which we  Append the current "quantum".
        true)
;;=> If we were able to find a fireable instruction,
;;    we issue "true".
        false)))

;; => Else we issue "false".
```

24. The following functions will help us prepare empty `locks` and `scheduled` maps, which are to be used by `progress-on-process!`:

```
(defn prepare-scheduled
  [processes]
  (into [] (->> processes
                (map (fn[p] {:process-id (:process-id p)
                            :instructions (into []
(->> (:instructions p)
(map (fn [i] (assoc i
:times [])))))})))))
;;=> We prepare "scheduled" as being the same thing as the
;;    "processes" map
;;    with empty ":times" vectors added.
```

```
(defn prepare-locks-for-a-p
  [a-process]
  (let [locks (filter #(= (:inst-type %) :lock )
                      (:instructions a-process))]
    (reduce (partial apply unlock) {} (map (fn [l] [(:process-id
a-process)
  (:inst-id l)])
                                      locks))))
;;=> A helper function that will prepare "locks" set to false for
;;    instructions related to a process"
(defn prepare-locks
  [processes]
  (reduce merge (map prepare-locks-for-a-p processes)))
;;=> Applying "prepare-locks-for-a-p", we generate locks for all
;;    processes  that would run concurrently.
```

25. Equipped with all these functions, we must address the problem of process selection for the allocation of each quantum of time. We must give each process an opportunity to access the scheduler quanta according to its priority. For this purpose, we will construct an infinite sequence of holding repetitions of a process ID as many times as their priority values. In this, a process with higher priority will always come before another with lower priority. Suppose we have process p1 with priority 3, process p2 with priority 2, and process p3 with priority 1, then a sequence presenting the cycling that we described previously would be:

    [p1 p1 p1 p2 p2 p3 p1 p1 p1 p2 p2 p3....]

26. As the time quantums flow, the scheduler will have to pick at each step an element, cycling through the weighted cycling list, which we just saw, to be sure it is fair toward the process's priority.

27. The following functions create the priority-weighted cycling process IDs:

```
(defn gen-processes-cycles
  [processes]
  (let [sorted-procs-by-prio (sort-by :priority > processes)
        procs-pattern (mapcat #(repeat (:priority %)
                                       %)
                              sorted-procs-by-prio)]
;;=> A pattern is a single repetition "priority" times of each
;;    process
    (cycle procs-pattern)))
;;=> Generates an infinite sequence like we described above.
```

28. Locking programs may lead to infinite waiting. To tackle this problem, we will set a time-out for our scheduler, which will be twice the time needed by all the processes if they were to be executed sequentially, one after the other. This function does just that:

```
(defn process-sequential-time
  [a-process]
  (let [instructions (a-process :instructions)
        inst-types (map :inst-type instructions)
        lengths (map #(get insts-effort %) inst-types)]
    (reduce + lengths)))
;;=> We get instruction-types, grab the efforts from the "insts-
;;    effort"
;;    map and sum them all up using reduce.
```

29. Finally, we can write our scheduler. While there are incomplete processes left to be scheduled and before the current quantum reaches time-out, the scheduler will cycle the weighted processes cycles, pick one process, and call `progress-on-a-process!` on it. Note that we launch this on several programs as we are implementing time-sharing to do multithreading:

```
(defn schedule-programs
  [language programs]
;;=> programs are maps : {:program "the textual program",
;;   :process-id the-process-id
;;   :priority the-process-priority }
  (let [processes (into [] (map #(fire-a-process language
                                               (:program %)
                                               (:process-id %)
                                               (:priority %))
programs))
;;=> Processes are constructed
        timeout (* 2 (reduce + (map process-sequential-time
                                    processes)))
;;=> "timeout" is the total length of all processes executed one
;;    after the other.
        locks (ref (prepare-locks processes))
        scheduled (ref (prepare-scheduled processes))
        processes-cycles (gen-processes-cycles processes)]
;;=> We prepare "locks" and "scheduled" refs, and the weighted
;;    process repetitions that the scheduler will have to cycle
;;    through
(loop [quantum 0
           remaining-processes processes-cycles]
;;=> We loop
        (if (and (more-incomplete-processes? (scheduled-processes-
parts @scheduled))
```

```
                    (< quantum timeout))
            (do
              (progress-on-process! locks scheduled
                                    (first remaining-processes)
                                    quantum)
      ;;=> progress on the selected process, with current "quantum"
              (recur (inc quantum)
                      (next remaining-processes)))
      ;;=> Go to next iteration, incrementing quantum and cycling
      ;;=> through the The weighted processes cycles.
              @scheduled)))
```

Now, let's define two random programs and see how they perform. First, define them in your REPL:

```
(def programs
[{:priority 3,
  :program
  "heavy-op op1;light-op op2;lock l1;medium-op op3;unlock l1;",
  :process-id :pr1}
 {:priority 1,
  :program "lock l1;medium-op op4;unlock l1;medium-op op5;",
  :process-id :pr2}])
```

Now, launch `schedule-programs`:

```
(p  (schedule-programs r3-language programs))
```

By launching it, you'll get the following output:

```
[{:process-id :pr1,
  :instructions
  [{:times [0 1 2 4 5 6 8 9 10 12],
    :inst-type :heavy-op,
    :inst-id "op1"}
   {:times [13 14], :inst-type :light-op, :inst-id "op2"}
   {:times [16], :inst-type :lock, :inst-id {:lock "l1"}}
   {:times [17 18 20 21 22], :inst-type :medium-op, :inst-id "op3"}
   {:times [24], :inst-type :unlock, :inst-id {:unlock "l1"}}]}
 {:process-id :pr2,
  :instructions
  [{:times [3], :inst-type :lock, :inst-id {:lock "l1"}}
```

```
{:times [7 11 15 27 31], :inst-type :medium-op, :inst-id "op4"}
{:times [35], :inst-type :unlock, :inst-id {:unlock "11"}}
{:times [39 43 47 51 55], :inst-type :medium-op, :inst-id "op5"}]}]
```

Simulating a call stack using arrays

A call stack is a data structure that is built when a program runs. As function calls keep coming
in, the information regarding their code is arranged in frames, that is, a frame per call or
variable evaluation. And these frames are stacked up. The program execution is then a matter of
"unwinding" these frames, that is, after a frame at the top of the stack has been evaluated, it is
unstacked and the process resumes at the new frame that is now at the top of the call stack.

Here we will observe a simple rule to unwind: as the execution goes, if we unstack a variable, we
store it, and when we encounter a function call to unstack, we store the return value of its call
and pass to it the parameters that we've stored so far. The next figure explains this process:

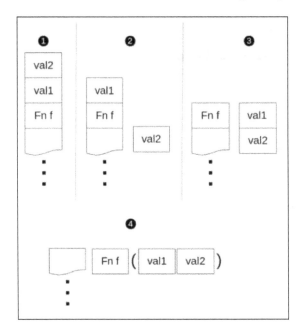

Unwinding the frames in a call Stack

How to do it...

1. First of all, let's define our `ns` (namespace) incorporating all Clojure facilities that we will use:

```
(ns recipe4.core
  (:require [instaparse.core :as insta])
;;=> To parse our programs
  (:require [clojure.zip :as z])
;;=> To walk and process parse trees
  (:require [clojure.pprint :refer :all])
;;=> To pretty print results
  (:require [clojure.walk :as walk]))
;;=> To transform some nodes
;;    in our programs' parse trees
```

2. We'll also alias `clojure.pprint/pprint` so that we can easily pretty-print the results of our computations:

```
(def p pprint)
```

3. We'll design a minimal language that will be parsed with `instaparse`.

 Instaparse (`https://github.com/engelberg/instaparse`) is a parser generator written in Clojure. Explaining the mechanism of Instaparse is beyond the scope of this book, but you should know it handles **context-free grammars** (**CFG**), and generates parse trees of your input programs according to these grammar concepts.

4. Our language will only be able to understand function calls. You can think of it as a kind of Lisp, but with no prefix notation; you can write your functions using the old mathematical way in this. Besides, our language is able to understand function declarations. Here is an example of what a program in this language looks like:

```
decl-fn f(x,y){
  plus(x,y);
};
plus(f(1,2),f(3,4));
```

5. The functions without declarations are considered `primitive` or `library` functions in our programs.

6. Here is the `instaparse` grammar that is able to parse programs written in our minimal language:

```
(def r4-language
 "S =  ((FN-CALL|FN-DECL) <FN-SEP>)*
  FN-CALL = <optional-whitespace> ID <optional-whitespace>
              <left-paren> PARAMS-LIST <right-paren>
  PARAMS-LIST = <optional-whitespace> (ID|FN-CALL)
                          (<optional-whitespace> <PARAMS-SEP>
                           <optional-whitespace> (ID|FN-CALL))*
  FN-DECL = <optional-whitespace> 'decl-fn'
                      <whitespace> ID <optional-whitespace>
                       <left-paren> ARGS-LIST <right-paren>
                      <optional-whitespace>
                      <left-curly>  FN-DECL-BODY <right-curly>
  ARGS-LIST = <optional-whitespace> ID
                        (<optional-whitespace> <PARAMS-SEP>
                         <optional-whitespace> ID)*
  FN-DECL-BODY = (FN-CALL <FN-SEP>)*
  left-paren = '('
  right-paren = ')'
  left-curly = '{'
  right-curly = '}'
  ID = #'[a-zA-Z0-9]+'
  whitespace = #'\\s+'
  optional-whitespace = #'\\s*'
  FN-SEP = <optional-whitespace> ';' <optional-whitespace>
  PARAMS-SEP = <optional-whitespace> ',' <optional-whitespace>")
```

7. Note that identifiers between angle brackets will not be shown in the parse tree, so there's no use of referring to `white-space` tags, for instance.

8. Let's see what the parse tree of the program we previously wrote looks like. Issue the following code in your REPL:

```
(p  (insta/parse  (insta/parser r4-language) "
decl-fn f(x,y){
                         plus(x,y);
                         };
plus(f(1,2),f(3,4));"))
```

9. After this step, you'll get the following output:

```
[:S
 [:FN-DECL
  "decl-fn"
  [:ID "f"]
  [:ARGS-LIST [:ID "x"] [:ID "y"]]
  [:FN-DECL-BODY
   [:FN-CALL [:ID "plus"] [:PARAMS-LIST [:ID "x"] [:ID "y"]]]]]
 [:FN-CALL
  [:ID "plus"]
  [:PARAMS-LIST
   [:FN-CALL [:ID "f"] [:PARAMS-LIST [:ID "1"] [:ID "2"]]]
   [:FN-CALL [:ID "f"] [:PARAMS-LIST [:ID "3"] [:ID "4"]]]]]]
```

10. Now we'll use the `instaparse` and `transform` functions to provide a more convenient representation of our parsed program. `transform` function replaces particular tags in the parse tree, applying a function to the rest of elements in the vector that contains those tags. Here is how we want to transform the parse trees:

```
(defn gen-program
  [parser program]
  (into [] (insta/transform
             {:S (fn [ & args] args)
              :FN-CALL (fn [fn-id params] [:FN-CALL
                                           (fn-id 1)
                                           params])
              :PARAMS-LIST (fn [& params] (into [] params) )
              :FN-DECL (fn [_ decl-fn-id  args body] [:FN-DECL
(decl-fn-id 1)
                                                      args body])
              :ARGS-LIST (fn [& args] (into [] args))
              :FN-DECL-BODY (fn [& body] (into [] body))}
             (parser program))))
```

11. To better understand what this function does you can refer to its output, which is as follows. Input the following code in to your REPL:

```
(p (gen-program (insta/parser r4-language) "decl-fn f(x,y){
   plus(x,y);
};
plus(f(1,2),f(3,4));" ))
```

12. After completing this step, you'll get the following output:

```
[[:FN-DECL
  "f"
  [[:ID "x"] [:ID "y"]]
  [[:FN-CALL "plus" [[:ID "x"] [:ID "y"]]]]]
 [:FN-CALL
  "plus"
  [[:FN-CALL "f" [[:ID "1"] [:ID "2"]]]
   [:FN-CALL "f" [[:ID "3"] [:ID "4"]]]]]]]
```

13. With this representation of our program, we first need to know which functions are declared:

```
(defn get-fn-decls
  [program]
  (->> program
       (filter #(= :FN-DECL (get % 0)))
;;=> Take only instructions with :FN-DECL tag
       (into []))))
```

14. Complementary to this function, we need a function that tells us which instructions (function calls) we have in our program:

```
(defn get-instructions
  [program]
  (->> program
       (filter #(not= :FN-DECL (get % 0)))
;;=> Take only instructions with no :FN-DECL tag.
       (into []))))
```

15. Now we will focus on how to translate declared function calls. We need to exchange the reference to such calls with the bodies of declaration, in which we inject the parameters passed along with the call. Let's first see the declaration of a particular function:

```
(defn get-fn-id-decl
  [fn-decls fn-id]
  (->> fn-decls
       (filter #(= (get % 1)
                   fn-id))
;;=> Returns the fn-decl that matches the passed fn-id.
       (first)))
;;=> This function will return 'nil' if there is no
;;   declaration found for it.
```

16. Now we are going to implement `call-fn`, which is a function that does the actual translation of a function call using its declaration (if we ever find any) and passed parameters:

```
(defn call-fn
  [fn-decl fn-call]
  (let [decl-args-list (fn-decl 2)
;;=> we get the args in the declaration
        decl-body (fn-decl 3)
;;=> We get the body of the declaration.
        fn-call-params (fn-call 2)]
;;=> We get the passed parameters
    (if (not (= (count decl-args-list) (count fn-call-params)))
      [:arity-error-in-calling (fn-decl 1 )]
;;=> If the count of parameters and args mismatch, we say we have
an arity error
      (let [replacement-map (zipmap decl-args-list fn-call-params)]
;;=> we prepare a replacement map for 'postwalk-replace':
;;   zipmap builds a map containing keys from the first seq
;;   'decl-args-list' and vals from the second one 'fn-call-params'.
        (walk/postwalk-replace replacement-map decl-body)))))
;;=> 'postwalk-replace' will then change in 'decl-body' the
;;       arguments 'decl-args-list' by corresponding paramters in
;;       'fn-call-params'
```

17. Next, we will do the actual translation of the declared function calls and leave the non-declared functions as they are, assuming that they are `primitive` or `library` functions. This is why we called the `expand-to-primitive-calls` function:

```
(defn expand-to-primitive-calls
[program]   ;;=> A program generated with 'gen-program'
(let  [fn-decls (get-fn-decls program)
       instructions (get-instructions program)
    ;;=> preparing function declarations and instructions .
       zpr (z/vector-zip instructions)]
       ;;=> A zipper to walk instructions.
  (loop [result instructions

;;=> We initially have our result set to be our instructions.
         loc (-> zpr z/down)]
    (if (-> loc z/end?)
      result
;;=> end of recursion. If no more nodes to visit, we emit result.
      (let [current-node (-> loc z/node)]
;;=> We store current node
```

```
                  (if (= (get current-node 0 :FN-CALL))
;;=> If it is a function call
(if-let [the-decl (get-fn-id-decl fn-decls (get current-node 1))]
           ;;=> and it has a declaration associated with it
              (recur (walk/postwalk-replace {(-> loc z/node)
                                             (call-fn the-decl
current-node)}

                                                  result )
                        (->  loc z/next))
     ;;=> we recur replacing this current-nod with
     ;; the function declaration along with the parameters.
              (recur result (-> loc z/next)))
  ;;=> else we recur leaving the function as is considering it
  ;; to be 'primitive'.
              (recur result (-> loc z/next))))))))
  ;;=> or we recur leaving the instruction as is, because here
  ;; we only have a variable evaluation.
```

18. At this particular point we are able to construct a call stack for an instruction:

```
(defn a-call-stack
  [a-call]
  (let [zpr (z/vector-zip a-call)]
;;=> A zipper to walk our call.
    (loop [result []
           loc (-> zpr z/down)]
     (if (-> loc z/end?)
        result
;;=> End of the recursion, we emit result.
        (let [current-node (-> loc z/node)]
;=> we store the current node.
          (recur (if (and
                      (not (vector? current-node))
                      (not= :FN-CALL current-node)
                      (not= :ID current-node))
;;=> If this is a literal, that is, not a vector, and not a tag,
(conj result {(-> loc z/left z/node) current-node})
;;=> I add it to the stack, along with the node at its left;
;;=> for instance, we'll have {:ID a-value}
;;   or {:FN-CALL a value}
                      result)
;; => Else we leave the stack as is.
                 (-> loc z/next)))))))
; and we go to the next node.
```

19. Finally, we will get to construct a stack for every instruction:

```
(defn program-call-stack
  [prog]
  (into []
        (map a-call-stack
             (expand-to-primitive-calls prog)))))
```

Let's see how it works. Type the following in to your REPL:

```
(p  (program-call-stack (gen-program (insta/parser r4-language)
"decl-fn f(x,y){
  plus(x,y);
};
plus(f(1,2),f(3,4));
f(4,5);" )))
```

The result of this would be:

```
[[{:FN-CALL "plus"}
  {:FN-CALL "plus"}
  {:ID "1"}
  {:ID "2"}
  {:FN-CALL "plus"}
  {:ID "3"}
  {:ID "4"}]
 [{:FN-CALL "plus"} {:ID "4"} {:ID "5"}]]
```

Here, the stack top comes last, as vectors in Clojure are way more efficiently accessed from the tail. This stack would be unwinded as follows:

1. This stack processes instruction 1.
2. Then it stores the value 4.
3. Stores the values 3,4.
4. Stores the value of plus("3","4").
5. Stores the values of 2, plus("3","4").
6. Stores the values of 1,2, plus("3","4").
7. Stores the values of plus("1","2"), plus("3","4").
8. Stores the values of plus(plus("1","2"), plus("3","4")).

9. Instruction 1 finishes returning `plus(plus("1","2"),plus("3","4"))`.

10. Then it processes instruction 2.

11. Stores the value `5`.

12. Stores the values `4,5`.

13. Stores the value of `plus ("4","5")`.

14. Instruction 2 finishes returning the value of `plus ("4","5")`.

2

Alternative Linked Lists

In this chapter, we will discuss the following recipes, related to linked lists:

- ▶ Building a doubly linked XOR list
- ▶ Speeding up access to linked list elements
- ▶ Building a simple shift-reduce parser
- ▶ Implementing a skew binary random-access list

Building a doubly linked XOR list

In a linked list, we chain elements to the next occurring item by storing a reference in each element. Hence, you can only walk linked lists in a single direction, accessing at each step the information about where to look for the next cell. Take the example of Clojure, where `seq` is implemented as a linked list. Here, to walk this data structure, you can only call `rest` to access tail elements, and you have no means of moving backwards.

One way to add backward-moving capability to linked lists is to turn them into doubly linked lists. Just as you store the information in each cell about the next one, you would also have to store a reference to the previous element. However, you'd have to store two references in each cell, doubling your needs in memory to store pointers to elements.

When you cannot afford to bear this memory overhead, but require the ability to traverse a list in both directions, a doubly linked XOR list can be used. Such a list is constructed by storing, along with each cell, the result of applying bitwise XOR to the preceding item and the next one's address. If *A*, *B*, *C*, and *D* are some of the elements of a linked list, in *B* we'll store *xor-link(B)* = *A⊕C* and *C xor-link(C)= B⊕D* as:

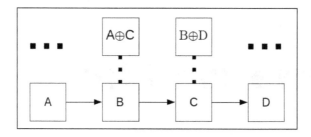

Getting the address of the element to the left or right of a particular cell is a matter of applying an XOR operation to the XOR link stored in that cell, along with the element to its right if we're moving to the left, or the element to its left if we're moving in the other direction. Consider the following bitwise XOR properties:

▸ *A⊕(B⊕C) = A⊕B⊕C*

▸ *A⊕B = B⊕A*

▸ *A⊕A = 0*

▸ *0⊕A = A*

So, if you are in *B* and want to move right to the next element, you need to retrieve a reference, as follows:

A⊕xor-link(B) = A⊕(A⊕C) = A⊕A⊕C = 0⊕C = C

Being in *C*, we get to the previous element, to its left, by calculating:

D⊕xor-link(C) = D⊕(B⊕D)=D⊕ (D⊕B)=D⊕D⊕B=0⊕B=B

So, to walk a doubly linked XOR list either way, we'll need one single register variable containing the previously visited element along with the XOR links stored in each cell.

How to do it...

1. We will start with the simply linked lists and generate the XOR links afterwards. We'll use our own implementation, so that we can inspect the addresses of the elements and understand the later computations. Here is the structure that we designed:

```
[{:address 0, :next 1, :id :cell0}
 {:address 1, :next 2, :id :cell1}
 {:address 2, :next nil, :id :cell2}]
```

2. Now, we have to define some functions to navigate through the linked list:

```
(defn r5-ll-first
  [llist]
  (first llist))      ;;=> returns first element of the list
(defn r5-ll-next
  ([llist] (r5-ll-next llist
                       (r5-ll-first llist)))
;;=> the next of a llist with no argument returns  the first
;;   element of the list
  ([llist cell]
     (if-let [next-cell-address (get cell :next)]
       (get llist next-cell-address)
  nil)))
;;=> Given a cell, we access the :next pointer and return
;;   the element at that address.

(defn r5-ll-last
  [llist]
  (loop [cell (r5-ll-first llist)]
    (if (= nil (get cell :next))
      cell
;;=> This is the last element, no next for it.
      (recur (r5-ll-next llist cell)))))
;; else we continue with next cell.
```

3. We'll need a function to retrieve the element positioned before a particular item. We do not cheat by using array elements; we traverse the list from the beginning until we find an element whose :next pointer refers to our parameter cell:

```
(defn get-before-cell
  [llist
   cell]
  (let [cell-address (get cell :address)]
    (loop [current (r5-ll-first llist)]
      (if (= (get current :next) cell-address)
        current
;;=> We found it.
        (if (= nil (get current :next))
          nil
;;=> We got to the end, so we were unable to find it.
          (recur (r5-ll-next llist current)))))))
;;=> We carry on with the next cell.
```

4. With these utility functions in hand, we are able to write the generation of a doubly linked list properly:

```
(defn gen-xor-llist
  [llist]
    (loop [result []
           current  (r5-ll-first llist)]
      (let [current-address (get current :address)
```

```
                          ;;=> We take current element address
                          after-current (r5-ll-next llist current)
                          after-current-address  (if-let [nxt-addr (get current
:next)]
                                                     nxt-addr
                                                     0)
;;=> Next one's address
                          before-current (get-before-cell llist
                                                      current)
                          before-current-address (if before-current
                                            (before-current :address)
                                    0)]
;;=> And address of the element before.
            (if (= nil current)
;;=> If at after the last element,
;;    we get the addresses of last and first cells
;;    in the original linked list and those
;;    in the xor-linked list
            (let [the-last (r5-ll-last llist)
                    before-last-in-ll (get-before-cell llist the-last)
                    before-last-in-ll-address (get before-last-in-ll
:address)
                    the-last-in-xor-list (peek result)
                    the-first-in-ll (r5-ll-first llist)
                    the-first-in-xor-list (first result)]
                (->> result
                    (replace {the-last-in-xor-list
                                {:is-last true
                                 :id (the-last-in-xor-list :id)
                                 :address (the-last-in-xor-list
:address)
                                 :xor-link before-last-in-ll-address}})
                    (replace {the-first-in-xor-list
                                {:is-first true
                                 :id (the-first-in-xor-list :id)
                                 :address (the-first-in-xor-list
:address)
                                 :xor-link (the-first-in-ll :next)}}))))
;;=> We store in the xor-link of the first cell the address
;;    of the next element, so we can do get to it by computing
;;    0 xor next-address. Same logic applies to the last element,
;;    in whose xor-link we put the address of the previous cell.
            (let [xor-link (bit-xor before-current-address
                                    after-current-address)
;;=> Computing the xor link and the new cell for the
;;    other steps of the recursion
                    new-cell {:id (get current :id)
                              :address (get current :address)
                              :xor-link xor-link}]
                (recur (conj result new-cell)
```

```
;;=> And we construct the xor-list as we go through the list.
                   (r5-ll-next llist current)))))))
```

5. Finally, let's implement `get-xor-after`, with which we will be able to navigate our XOR linked list, which is generated by the previous function from left-to-right or right-to-left:

```
(defn get-xor-after
  [xor-llist
   cell-id
;;=> The cell ID you want to
;;    start moving to next element
;;    from
   direction]
;;=> :right or :left
     (loop [current (cond
                      (= direction :right) (first xor-llist)
;;=> Going right, begin from first element
                      (= direction :left) (peek xor-llist))
;;=> Going left, we start with last one.
            previous-address 0]
;;=> The registry we are going to use to store
;;    the address of the previous element we walked in.
        (let [next-cell-address (bit-xor previous-address
                                          (current :xor-link))
;;=> Computing the next address using xor-link
;;    and the registry.
              next-cell (get xor-llist next-cell-address)
;;=> And getting into it, while updating
;;    the registry
              new-previous-address (get current :address)]
          (if (or (and (= direction :right) (get current :is-last))
                  (and (= direction :left) (get current :is-first)))
              nil
;;=>  We are at the bounds of the list, there is
;;     no next to return in either direction
              (if (= cell-id (get current :id))
                  next-cell
;;=> Here we found a valid next,
;;    So we exit the recursion and return it
                  (recur next-cell
                         new-previous-address))))))
;;    else we carry on with the recursion.
```

Now, you'll be able to move left or right, starting from an element defined by the ID that you provide to the function:

```
(get-xor-after a-xor-llist :some-id :left)
(get-xor-after a-xor-llist :some-other-id :right)
```

Speeding up access to linked list elements

Searching for an element in a linked list is a very iteration-consuming task. For every such query, you'd have to start at the head of the list and jump from element to element using the next cell's references till you find the item you're looking for. This is a worst case $O(N)$ operation, which is quite expensive as it grows at the same time as the size of your data.

One thing that we can do about this is inspired by caching. Caching is about storing the most-accessed elements in a "close" place, drastically reducing the complexity of retrieving elements from sequential data structures.

As far as linked lists are concerned, we would store the most-accessed elements near the head of the list, as this would be the "closest" place for every linked list retrieval algorithm. Here, you'd always start from the beginning of the list to begin any traversal operation. This will be done by always storing the result of every element inquiry at the head of the list.

How to do it...

1. First of all, we need to come up with some utility functions:

```
(defn r6-ll-first
  [llist]
  (first llist))

(defn r6-ll-next
  ([llist] (r6-ll-next llist
                        (r6-ll-first llist)))
  ([llist cell]
    (if-let [next-cell-address (get cell :next)]
      (get llist next-cell-address)
      nil)))
;;=> First and next will allow us to traverse the list

(defn get-cell-by-id
```

```
  [llist
   cell-id]
  (loop [current (r6-ll-first llist)]
    (if (= cell-id (get current
                         :id))
      current
;;=> We got the Cell with the ID we're seeking
      (if (= nil (get current
                      :next))
        nil
;;=> We hit the end, the ID is not there
        (recur (r6-ll-next llist
                           current))))))
;;=> We carry-on with the next element

(defn get-before-cell
  [llist
   cell]
  (let [cell-address (get cell :address)]
    (loop [current (r6-ll-first llist)]
      (if (= (get current :next)
             cell-address)
;;=> This is the cell we are looking for
        current
        (if (= nil (get current :next))
          nil
;;=> We reached the end, so our cell must not be there.
          (recur (r6-ll-next llist
                             current)))))))
;;=> We recur with the next element
```

2. Now, we need to define a function to remove a cell from a linked list:

```
(defn remove-ll-element
  [llist
   cell-id]
  (let [cell (get-cell-by-id llist
                             cell-id)
        cell-address (get cell
                          :address)]
;;=> We have the cell to remove,
    (loop [llist-wo-cell []
```

```
                    current (r6-ll-first llist)]
          (if (= nil current)
            llist-wo-cell
            ;;=> Done with the recursion
            ;;   we return the result
            (let [current-address (get current :address)
                  next-address (get current :next)
                  new-address (if (> current-address
                                     cell-address)
                                (dec current-address)
                                current-address)
;;=> If the address occurs AFTER the
;;   element to be removed, we decrease it.
                  new-next-address (if (= nil next-address)
                                     nil
                                     (cond
                                       (> next-address cell-address)
                                         (dec next-address)
;;=> If next address comes after the element
;;   to be removed, we decrease it
                                       (< next-address cell-address)
next-address
                                       (= next-address cell-address)
                                         (if-let [nxt-c-addr (get
cell :next)]

(dec nxt-c-addr)
                    ;;=> We decrease it if it is
                    ;;   equal to the address to the cell
                    ;;   to be removed and if its next isn't
                    ;;   nil, else it is nil.

nil)))]
          (recur (if (= current cell)
                   llist-wo-cell  ;;=> We remove cell from result
                   (conj llist-wo-cell {:address new-address
                                        :id (current :id)
                                        :next new-next-address}))
                 ;;=> And add the new elements to result.
```

```
                       (r6-ll-next llist
                                current)))))))
        ;;=> And we go on with the next element.
```

3. Let's now define a function to move a given `cell-id` into the head of a linked list:

```
(defn move-cell-to-head
  [llist
   cell-id]
  (let [llist-wo-cell (remove-ll-element llist
                                         cell-id)
        ;;=> We begin by constructing a list
        ;; without the cells to remove, and incrementing
        ;; by one all cells addresses and pointers to next
        ;; elements in this list,
        llist-wo-cell-addrs+1 (loop [result []
                                     current (r6-ll-first llist-wo-cell)]
                                (if (= nil current)
                                  result
                                  (recur (conj result
                                               {:address (inc
                                                          (get current
:address))

                                                :next (if-let [nxt-addr
                                                               (get current
:next)]

                                                        (inc nxt-addr)
                                                        nil)
                                                :id (get current
                                                         :id)})
                                         (r6-ll-next llist-wo-cell
                                                     current)))))]
        ;;=> Then we return a list with the removed element
        ;;    at head position, and the rest of the list whose
        ;;    addresses have been incremented.
        (into [{:id cell-id
                :address 0
                :next 1}]
              llist-wo-cell-addrs+1)))
```

4. Finally, we have to implement the caching search function. We'll use an atom to store, after each search operation, the new linked list with the fetched element at head:

```clojure
(defn search-for-cell-by-id!
  [llist-atom
   cell-id]
  (loop [current (r6-ll-first @llist-atom)]
    (if (= current nil)
      nil ;;=> Reached the end and did not
          ;; find the element
      (if   (= (current :id)
               cell-id)
        ;;=> If we find it,
        (let [_ (swap! llist-atom
                       move-cell-to-head
                       (current :id))]
          ;;=> We update the atom
          current)
        ;;=> And return the found element
        (recur (r6-ll-next @llist-atom
                           current))))))
  ;;=> Else we recur with the next elements
```

We can now see our caching search in action. Let's define an atom that refers to a linked list:

```clojure
(def llist-atom (atom
                  [{:address 0 :id :cell0 :next 1}
                   {:address 1 :id :cell1 :next 2}
                   {:address 2 :id :cell2 :next 3}
                   {:address 3 :id :cell3 :next nil}]))
```

Now, we'll search for `:cell2`:

```clojure
(search-for-cell-by-id! llist-atom :cell2)
;; => {:address 2, :next 3, :id :cell2}
```

The contents of our `llist-atom` are:

```clojure
(clojure.pprint/pprint @llist-atom)
[{:id :cell2, :address 0, :next 1}
 {:address 1, :next 2, :id :cell0}
 {:address 2, :next 3, :id :cell1}
 {:address 3, :next nil, :id :cell3}]
```

The `:cell2` element is placed at the top of the list, accelerating all subsequent searches to it.

Building a simple shift-reduce parser

A **shift-reduce parser** is a program that is generated from a grammar definition. It is a kind of state machine capable of doing two kinds of actions:

- ▸ Either it consumes a token from an input program, adding up a new state in a stack. This is called **shifting**.

- ▸ It recognizes that a rule of grammar has been fully matched, so it pops as many states from the stack as the rule contains and acknowledges that it recognized that particular rule, adding up an entry to the parse tree. This is known as **reducing**.

Given how these parsers operate, we'd say that they belong to the "bottom-up" parsing family. That is, they operate on input and deduce the parse outcome while traversing it, in contrast to the other way around, which is starting from the rules of grammar and finding structures in the program that obey them. Our parser will then operate on a linked list structure, consuming tokens one after another.

Now, a particular state of the parser depicts the situation it has come to after having consumed some tokens of the input program at a particular point of the parse process. Consider for example the following grammar code:

```
S=B+C
A=id
B=id
```

We call the rule identifiers S, A, and B as nonterminals. The symbols that are not defined by a rule such as id are called terminals.

The initial state related to our grammar would be:

```
S=.B+C
B=.id
C=.id
```

Here, we did not consume anything, yet the point denotes the position that we process in a specific grammar rule. If we input a symbol from our input program, and if it is id, we would reach the following state:

```
B=id.
```

Now, the parser recognizes that it can reduce B. We input the B=id. rule from the states stack and apply transition *B* to state A=.B+C, applying transition B, thus attaining the state:

```
A=B.+C
```

Now, the parse tree contains [B id]. The process goes on until it reduces the starting rule, S.

The parser is then constructed as:

1. You need to build all possible states.

2. You need to find all grammar symbols, terminals, and nonterminals.

3. You need to build a transition table that is capable, given a state, and a symbol (terminal or nonterminal) to tell the parser which state to go to next. This is done for all possible states and grammar symbols.

How is the transition table constructed? Given a state, which is represented as a rule with a point describing the position being processed by the parser (as in *A=B.+C*), consuming a symbol makes that point advance by a position. If the point lands before a non-terminal symbol, the rule defining that very non-terminal (with the point at the beginning of a rule definition) is added to that state.

The parsing process is rolled out following this algorithm as:

1. If reducing is possible, input from the states stack as many elements as the rule that we are reducing by contains; let's call this number *n*. Advance from the state that is left at the top using the nonterminal we just used. Populate the parse tree by assigning to it the same nonterminal *n* elements at the top of that parse tree.

2. Otherwise, shift one token from the input and go to the state that this token would lead to, starting from the state that is currently at the top of the stack.

3. If at any moment it is impossible to go to the target state, raise a parse error.

> A deeper explanation of the parsing theory is beyond the scope of this book. A good introduction to the subject can be found at `http://dragonbook.stanford.edu/lecture-notes/Stanford-CS143/08-Bottom-Up-Parsing.pdf`.

How to do it...

1. We'll first have to import some Clojure facilities. Here is our `ns` declaration:

```
(ns recipe7.core
  (:require [clojure.string :refer (split split-lines trim escape)])
  (:require [clojure.zip :as z]))
```

2. To define our rules, we will use two vectors. The first one will depict the part before the parsing point and the second will represent the symbols that come after that point, for example, if we consider the rule `S=.A+B` we would represent it using the following vector:

```
[S [] [A "+" B]]
```

3. Now, we'll have to b parse our grammar and generate vectors that associate rules with their definitions:

```
(defn parse-grammar
  [grammar]
  (let [lines (split-lines grammar)
  ;;=> Taking the input line by line
        lines-w-rule-names (->> lines
                                (map #(split  % #"=") )
  ;;=> splitting by the '=' symbol
                                (map (fn[[r b]] [(trim  r)
                                                (split (trim b)
                                                      #"\s+")]))
  ;;=> and then by space
                                (into [])))]
    lines-w-rule-names))

;; to get the [Rule [symbol1 …]] vectors
```

4. We will yield all the possible states or configurating sets as per the parsing theory terminology. Note that here we put them all under the same buckets, as individual states will be automatically generated later when we compute the transition table:

```
(defn gen-configs-from-def
  [v]
  (loop [result [[[] v]]
         before-point []
         after-point v]
    (if (empty? after-point)
      result
      ;;=> We are done with this definition
    (let [new-before-point (conj before-point (first after-point))
          new-after-point (into [] (next after-point))]
        ;;=> we advance the point, removing one symbol
        ;;    from the after-vector and putting it in
        ;;    the before-vector
        (recur
          ;;  then we advance with the next possible configuration
          (conj result [new-before-point
                        new-after-point])
          new-before-point
          new-after-point)))))

(defn gen-a-configurating-set
  [[rule definition]]
  (let [def-configs (gen-configs-from-def definition)]
```

```
;;=> We generate all configurations
;; with the rule name
(into [] (map (fn [def-config]
                [rule def-config])
              def-configs))))

(defn configurating-sets
  [parsed-grammar]
  (into []
        ;;=> We generate all configurating sets
        ;;   [rule [possible configuration...]]
        ;;     putting them in the same bucket
        (mapcat #(gen-a-configurating-set %)
                                          parsed-grammar)))
```

5. In the following code, we will focus on our grammar symbols:

```
(defn non-terminal?
[parsed-grammar
 symbol]
(loop [remaining parsed-grammar]
  ;;=> For each rule of our grammar
  (if (seq remaining)
    (let [current (first remaining)]
      (if (= symbol (get current 0))
        true
        ;;=> If the given symbol is at
        ;;    first place of one vector,
        ;;     it is considered as a non-terminal
        (recur (rest remaining))))
                ;;=> we check with the next rule
      false))) ;;=> we ended the recursion, hence
               ;; we were not able to match symbol
               ;; with a rule definition:
               ;; symbol is a terminal
(defn grammar-symbols
  [parsed-grammar]
  (let [zpr (z/vector-zip parsed-grammar)]
    (loop [symbols #{}
           loc (-> zpr z/down)]
      ;;=> We will inspect the rules
      ;; with a zipper
      (if (-> loc z/end?)
        symbols
;;=> The walk has ended, return symbols
```

```
(let [current-node (-> loc z/node)]
  (if (= (class current-node) String)
    ;;=> If we caught a grammar literal
    ;;   we add it to the result set
    (recur (conj symbols current-node)
           (-> loc z/next))
    ;;=> else we go deeper in the
    ;; rules tree without appending
    ;; to the result set
    (recur symbols
           (-> loc z/next))))))))))
```

6. We need to generate the configurating sets resulting from a single configurating set that consumes a symbol. Remember that this advances the point in the configurating set, and if while doing so the point lands before another nonterminal, it appends to the result the rule that defines this new terminal with a point at the very beginning:

```
(defn get-conf-sets-if-point-at-non-terminal
  [config-sets
   non-terminal]
  (into []
        ;;=> What are the rules defining
        ;;   this non terminal and having the
        ;;   point at the beginning of the
        ;;   definition ?
        (filter (fn[[r d]]
                  (and (= r non-terminal)
                       (empty? (get d 0))))
                config-sets)))

(defn point-at
  [[rule-name definition]]
  ;;=> Where is the point in
  ;;   this configurating set?
  (first (get definition 1)))

(defn cset-to-cset-transition
  [config-sets
   a-config-set
   a-symbol]
  (let [this-rule-name (get a-config-set 0)
        this-def (get a-config-set 1)
        this-def-before-point (this-def 0)
        this-def-after-point (this-def 1)]
    ;;=> Gathering information about the configurating
```

```
;;    set
(if (not=  a-symbol (first this-def-after-point))
  nil
  ;;=> This configurating set point cannot advance
  ;;   with this symbol
  (let [new-def-before-point (conj this-def-before-point
                                        a-symbol)
     new-def-after-point (into [] (rest this-def-after-point))
        new-config-set [this-rule-name [new-def-before-point
                                            new-def-after-point]]
        ;;=> What would the new configurating set be?
        new-config-exists? (some #(= new-config-set %)
                                    config-sets)]
        ;;=> Does it exist in the valid configurating sets?
     (if new-config-exists?
       new-config-set
       [:error (str "Symbol " a-symbol " not leading
anywhere!")])))))))


(defn state-to-state-given-a-symbol
  [parsed-grammar
   config-sets
   start-state
;;=> A state is a vector of configurating sets
   a-symbol]
  (let [direct-tr-state (->> start-state
                        (map #(cset-to-cset-transition config-sets
                                                        %

a-symbol))
                             (filter (partial not= nil))
                             (into []))
     ;;=> First we compute the state as the configurating sets
     ;;    immediately available by advancing the points
     added-states (->> (map  point-at
                             direct-tr-state)
                        (filter (partial  non-terminal?
                                                parsed-grammar))
                        (mapcat (partial
                        get-conf-sets-if-point-at-non-terminal
                                            config-sets)))]
     ;; And then we compute the states generated
     ;; The point landing in any non terminal state
  (into direct-tr-state added-states)))
```

7. Now, we are able to design a function that will tell us which transitions are possible from one state:

```
(defn all-transitions-from-state
  [parsed-grammar
   config-sets
   start-state]
  (let [all-symbols (grammar-symbols parsed-grammar)]
    (->> all-symbols
         (map (fn [symbol] (let [transition
                                  (state-to-state-given-a-symbol
                                    parsed-grammar
                                    config-sets
                                    start-state
                                    symbol)]
                ;; => We apply state-to-state for every symbol
                ;;    Of the grammar, starting from start state
                             (if ((comp not empty?) transition)
                ;;=> And we issue a map containing
                ;; a start-state, a transition symbol
                ;; and the state we'd be in applying
                ;; symbol to start-state
                               {:start-state start-state
                                :transition symbol
                                :end-state transition} ))))
         (filter (comp not nil?))
         (into []))))
```

8. Now, we are going to construct the transition table. First, we will devise a function to compute the starting state from a grammar and then we will build the actual table upon it:

```
(defn initial-state
  [config-sets]
  (into []
        ;;=> Initial state is built by
        ;;    keeping only rules with
        ;;    before-point vectors empty
        (filter (fn [[r d]]
                  (empty? (get d 0)))
                config-sets)))

(defn transition-table
  [parsed-grammar
   config-sets
   state0]
```

```
      (let [all-transitions-for-grammar
   (partial all-transitions-from-state
                                      parsed-grammar
                                      config-sets)]
     ;;=> We produce a partial function for commodity
     (loop [result (all-transitions-for-grammar state0)
            new-states (into [] (map :end-state result))]
       ;;=> We begin by computing the new states reached from
       ;;    state0
       (if (every? empty? new-states)
         result
         ;;=> If no new new-states, we are done.
         ;;    we emit result
       (let [new-transitions (mapcat all-transitions-for-grammar
                                     new-states)]
         ;;=> Else, we compute other states that'd be
         ;;    attained from these freshly computed new states
         ;;    recurring using them
         (recur (into result (filter (comp not empty?)
                                     new-transitions))
                (map :end-state
                     new-transitions)))))))
```

9. We'll then define a function that, given a transition table and symbol, will be able to tell us in which state the parser will be. Note that we can define our symbols as regular expressions in our grammar. So, we must define a special character escaping function beforehand, so that the regular expression matcher does not throw an error while interpreting our input grammar. These two functions are self-explanatory:

```
(defn escape-special-chars
  [s]
  (if (= \[  (first s))
    s
    (escape
     s
     {\+   "\\+"
      \*   "\\*"
      \?   "\\?"
      \^   "\\^"
      \|   "\\|"
      \&   "\\&"
      \(   "\\("
      \)   "\\)"
      \[   "\\["
      \]   "\\]"
```

```
          \{   "\\{"
          \}   "\\}"}))))

    (defn goto-state
      [tr-table
       start-state
       transition]
      (->> tr-table
           (filter  #(and  (= (get % :start-state)
                              start-state)
    (re-matches (re-pattern (escape-special-chars (get %
    :transition)))
                                              transition)))
           (first)
           :end-state))
```

10. Then, we design a function that determines whether a particular state is reduceable, that is, whether the point is at the very end of the rule definition in the configurating set; in our representation, the second vector is empty:

```
(defn verify-reduceable
  [state]
  (if-let [the-reduceable  (->> state
                               (filter #(let [rule-name (get % 0)
                                              definition (get % 1)
                                              before-point (get
definition 0)
                                              after-point (get
definition 1)]
                                          (if (empty? after-point)
true
                                              false)))
                               (first))]
    ;;=> If in our state there is one definition having the point
    ;;    at the end, that is, having the second vector empty,
    ;;    we consider it as reduceable, and return a map containing
    ;;    the name of the reducing rule and the number of symbols
    ;;    to reduce by, that is, the count of the contents of
    ;;    the first vector of the definition.
    ;;    Else, we return nil.
    {:reducing-rule (get the-reduceable 0)
     :nb-symbols-to-pop (count (get (get the-reduceable 1) 0))}
            nil))
```

11. We'll have to have a special version of `peek` and `pop`, which will be able to operate on `n` elements at a time. These are self-explanatory:

```
(defn pop-n
  [n v]
  (loop [times 0
         popped v]
    (if (or  (= times n)
             (empty? popped))
      popped
      (recur (inc times)
             (pop popped)))))


(defn peek-n
  [n v]
  (loop [result []
         times 0
         popped v]
    (if (or  (= times n)
             (empty? popped))
      result
      (recur (into [(peek popped)] result)
             (inc times)
             (pop popped)))))
```

12. Finally, we are able to write our main parser function! This takes a grammar and an input program and generates a parse tree or any parse error that it might have run into. At every iteration, the function will try to reduce else to shift. Whenever it notices that it has reduced the rule `S`, it exits and returns the parse tree. Note that the grammar literals must be separated by a space:

```
(defn parse-program
  [grammar
   program]
  (let [parsed-grammar (parse-grammar grammar)
        ;;=> We parse the grammar
        config-sets (configurating-sets parsed-grammar)
        ;;=> Generate the configurating-sets
        state0 (initial-state config-sets)
        ;;=> And the initial state
        tr-table (transition-table parsed-grammar
```

```
                        config-sets
                        state0)
        ;;=> We then build the transition table
        input (split program #"\s+")]
        ;;=> And lay the input program into a vector
        ;;    that we will traverse sequentially,
        ;;    as a linked list
    (loop [stack [state0]
;;=> The stake contains the initial state
          parse-tree []
;;=> The parse tree is empty
          remaining-input input
;;=> We initialize the input
          input-position 0
;;=> We'll keep track of input position for error reporting
          end? false]
;;=> this variable will be set to true
;;    whenever we detect we reduced rule 'S'
      (if end?
;;=> The parsing has ended with success, we return the parse tree
        parse-tree
;;    else we verify if the state at the top is reduce-able
        (if-let [reduce-transition (verify-reduceable (peek
stack))]
;;=> If it is, we update stack and parse tree as per the algorithm
          (let [reducing-rule (reduce-transition :reducing-rule)
            nb-symbols-to-pop (reduce-transition :nb-symbols-to-pop)
                stack-after-reducing (pop-n nb-symbols-to-pop
                                            stack)
;=> We pop n states from the stack
                stack-after-transition (conj stack-after-reducing
                                            (goto-state tr-table
                                                (peek
stack-after-reducing)

reducing-rule))
        ;;=> And go to the state determined by the transition of
        ;;    the state remaining at top with the reducing rule
name
```

```
                                new-end? (= reducing-rule "S")
;;=> Did we just reduce 'S'?
;;    Next time we stop.
                            new-parse-tree (if (not new-end?)
                                             (conj (pop-n nb-symbols-to-pop
                                                          parse-tree)
                                               [reducing-rule (peek-n
nb-symbols-to-pop

parse-tree)])
              ;;=> If I'm not at end, I wrap n last parsed symbols
              ;;    inside a vector with rule name as first element
              ;;    To construct the parse tree, along with the rest of
              ;;    Parse tree.
              ;;    Else I only wrap the symbols with a vector containing
              ;;    the 'S' rule
                              [reducing-rule (peek-n nb-symbols-to-pop
                                                     parse-tree)])]
                (recur stack-after-transition
                       new-parse-tree
                       remaining-input
                       input-position
                       new-end?))
        ;;=> And I recur
        ;;=> We will not reduce, so we are shifting
           (let [shifted-input (first remaining-input)
                 state-on-top (peek stack)]
             (if-let [new-state (goto-state tr-table
                                            state-on-top
                                            shifted-input)]
                ;;=> If there is a valid transition from the
                ;;    state at the top using the shifted token
                (recur (conj stack new-state)
                       (conj parse-tree shifted-input)
                       (rest remaining-input)
                       (inc input-position)
                       false)
        ;;=> We recur adding the new state
        ;;    and the shifted token to the parse tree
```

```
              (str "Parse Error: Unexpected symbol '"
                   shifted-input
                   "' at position "
                   input-position)))))))))
```

```
  ;;=> Else we emit a parse error
```

Let's see our parser in action now. Launch the code in your REPL (remember that all tokens must be separated by white spaces):

```
(parse-program "S=( A + B )
A=[a-z]*
B=[a-z]*"
"( abc + cde )")
```

The result of this is:

```
["S" ["(" ["A" ["abc"]] "+" ["B" ["cde"]] ")"]]
```

Implementing a skew binary random access list

Linked lists are traversed sequentially. To access an element, we need to begin at the top of the list and keep looking for references to the next cell and accessing it until we reach the item of our interest. In big O notation speak, access to an element in plain linked lists is a worst-case $O(N)$ operation, which is quite expensive.

If we want to implement efficient random access to the data that a linked list contains, that is, if we want to specify an index and get to it efficiently—just as in an array, we can consider arranging the same data in a binary search tree, providing for efficient lookup and insertion operations.

If you represent the subscripts of your nodes in a binary format, you'd have nodes connected to the subtrees that contain the elements that are next to them. Using such subscripts, you could navigate from a parent node to one of its children by simply adding a bit to its subscript at the least weight position, that is, to its extreme right. Say, some node is located at the subscript **1**. You'd navigate to its left child by accessing the subscript **10**, that is, its own subscript plus **0** to the right and you could navigate to its right child at the index **11** by following the same logic.

When descending the tree, deciding whether to go left or right at each step is a matter of looking for the value of that least significant bit; if it is **0**, you go left; otherwise, you go right. Let's assume that we want to access the contents of a cell with the index 5. 5 is written as **101** in binary. The path to it in a binary tree would be as shown in the following figure:

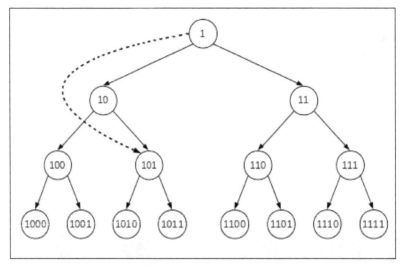

Getting to subscript 5 – 101 in a binary tree. (Numbers are subscripts).

However, we can do even better as far as computing elements' addresses is concerned, using a particular binary representation, the skew binary representation. In deed, at each step, computing the next element's addresses in a binary representation leads to a costly carry operation that would propagate all along the chain of bits representing every subscript, which is a quite tedious `O(log n)` worst-case operation. Thus, we can represent our indexes in the skew binary system, a nonstandard system that follows these steps:

1. Each position *n* is weighted by *(2n+1 – 1)*

2. We allow digits *0*, *1*, and *2* to represent our numbers; however, we only allow *2* to be the first non-zero digit

In case of incrementation, this representation does not incur any rippling carry operation. As we have the property *2(2n+1-1) + 1 = (2n+2-1)*, to increment a number, you have to follow a simple rule. If the first digit is *0* or *1*, we just increment it (which becomes *1* or *2*, respectively). If the number begins with *2*, we set the position that holds it to *0* and we increment the following digit. If we transpose that same idea to trees, we can fairly say that `consing`, that is, adding an element to the data structure, is analogous to incrementing a number.

To have a structure that is more capable of holding our data, we will use the sparse skew number representation, that is, we will only take into consideration the non-zero digits—we intend to have one tree per position (so we cannot keep the zeros!). Thus, we'll need to adjust the weights of these positions. What would *1* or *2* hold if there were no zeroes present? The following tables show how these numbers would look:

Number in the decimal format	Number in the skew binary representation (the least significant digit first)
1	1
2	2
3	01
4	11
5	21
6	02
7	001

Regarding the sparse representation, the following table shows what 1 would represent in each position (2 will be considered as the double of 1):

1 is in position in a binary skew representation of a number	Its weight : What value does it hold if all the other positions are set to 0
1	1
2	3
3	7
4	15
5	31
6	63
7	127

Given this representation, a decimal number would be represented by the weights of 1 (2 will be twice of 1 at the same position's weight), it contains like so:

Number in the decimal format	Number in the skew binary representation (the least significant digit first)	Number in the sparse skew binary representation (the least significant digit first)
1	1	[1]
2	2	[1,1]
3	01	[3]
4	11	[1,3]

Number in the decimal format	Number in the skew binary representation (the least significant digit first)	Number in the sparse skew binary representation (the least significant digit first)
5	21	[1,1,3]
6	02	[3,3]
7	001	[7]

The idea is to represent our structure as a list of couples, for example, (weight,tree). Each one of these couples contains a tree of the size weight, and its position gives the set of weight elements that come in that position.

Consing an element to a configuration is inspired by the incrementation of sparse skew binary represented numbers. For instance, if at any point in time we have 6 elements in our data, we would represent them as 2 trees of 3 elements, [3,3], and consing an element to it would lead us to a structure that contains 1 tree of 7 elements, that is, [7], as per the following figure:

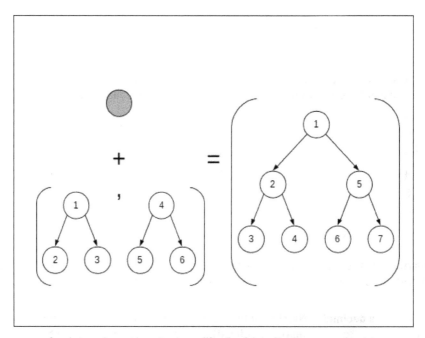

Consing an element in a structure of 6 cells of data. Numbers are subscripts

 A more elaborate explanation can be found in the original paper that explores these ideas, which is *Purely Functional Data Structures* by Chris Okasaki. This paper is available at http://www.cs.cmu.edu/~rwh/theses/okasaki.pdf.

How to do it...

1. Let's first declare our `ns` (namespace). We are going to make good use of `core.match`, which will make it easy for us to write our tree traversing code, thanks to pattern matching, that is, the process of recognizing particular structures in our input and triggering processes accordingly. Besides, you'll have to add the `core.match` dependency, `[org.clojure/core.match "0.3.0-alpha4"]`, inside your `:dependencies` section in your `project.clj` file:

```
(ns recipe8.core
  (:require [clojure.core.match :refer [match]]))
```

2. Our skew binary random access list will be a vector of `[weight,tree]`, as:

```
[[weight1 tree1] [weight2 tree2] .]
```

3. Let's begin by implementing `cons`:

```
(defn r8-cons
  [x ts]
  (match [ts] ;;=> Here we'll look into the structure
            ;;   of the tree to decide what to do.
        [[[w1 t1] [w2 t2] & ts*]] (if (= w1 w2)
                                    (into  [[(+ 1 w1 w2) (conj
[x] t1  t2 )]]
                                                ts*)
        ;;=> If if we have more than two couples
        ;;   and two first weights are equal,
        ;;   that is a 2. Analogous to the action
        ;;   of incrementing, which will set the
        ;;   2 at 0 and increment the next
        ;;   element, consing will create a
        ;;   single tree (thus setting this
        ;;   position to 0), made by setting the
        ;;   new element x as a root and appending
        ;;   to it the old two trees
        ;;   (just as if incrementing the next
            ;;   element), hence the new
            ;;   weight of (+ 1 w1 w2)
              (into [[1 x]] ts))
        ;;=> Else, we turn that same tree
        ;;   into a new one-thus having
        ;;   weight 1, and appending
        ;;   the whole old tree to a node
        ;;   only containing x. Just like
        ;;   incrementing an element
        ;;   that does not contain a 2.
```

```
    [ts]  (into [[1 x]] ts)))
;;=> This particular match clause
;;    is for the case when we don't have
;;    two couples (weight,tree), this is definitely not a 2
;;    so it resembles the story of incrementing a 0 or a 1.
```

4. We now design `head`:

```
(defn r8-head
  [ts]
  (match [ts]
         [[]] :empty
         ;;=> The head of an empty list
         ;;    raises an exception
         [[[1 a] & ts* ]] a
         ;;=> The head of a set beginning
         ;;    by a single element tree
         ;;    is that very element
         [[[w [a t1 t2]] & ts*]] a))
         ;;=> The head in general is the root
         ;;    of every first tree, here matched
         ;;    against an element tied to two sub-trees
```

5. We continue and move on to `tail`:

```
(defn r8-tail
  [ts]
  (match [ts]
         [[]] :empty
         ;;=> tail of an empty list raises an exception
         [[[1 a] & ts* ]] ts*
         ;;=> tail of a set beginning by a single element
         ;;    tree is everything that comes next
         [[[w [a t1 t2]] & ts*]] (into [ [(int (/ w 2)) t1]
                                         [(int (/ w 2)) t2]]
ts*)))
         ;;=> Tail of everything else is
         ;;    constructed out of the two subtrees
         ;;    that were tied by a root.
         ;;    We put them in the result set
         ;;    and set their weights to
         ;;    half the weight of the tree
         ;;    they used to form with root a.
```

6. Looking up an element in a skew binary access list involves two steps: finding out which of the arrays the element we are searching for is, and once we find it, traversing that tree to get to the element. We begin with the latter, r8-lookup-tree, as we'll need it for the former:

```
(defn r8-lookup-tree
  [w ts index]
  (match [w ts index]
        [1 a 0 ] a
        ;;=> Fetching subscript 0 with a w = 1 and a
        ;;    single element a yields a
        [1 a i] :index-error
        ;;=> i will not be 0 as we matched it in the
        ;;    previous match clause, so we are searching
        ;;    for something out of bound, hence we
        ;;    raise an exception
        [w [a t1 t2] 0] a
        ;;=> Searching for a first element in a set
        ;;    formed by a single tree returns the root
        ;;    of that same tree
        [w [a t1 t2] i] (if (<= i (int (/ w 2)))
                           (recur (int (/ w 2))
                                  t1
                                  (dec i))
                           ;;=> In general, to seek for an element
                           ;;    in a tree with weight w, we go
                           ;;    right if the subscript is less
                           ;;    than half the weight - t1
                           (recur (int (/ w 2))
                                  t2
                                  (- i 1 (int (/ w 2)))))))))
                           ;;=> Or we go left, t2
```

7. We can now use the previous function with r8-lookup:

```
(defn r8-lookup
  [ts index]
  (match [ts index]
        [[] i] :index-error
        ;;=> No element at all, raising an exception
        [[[w t] & ts*] i] (if (< i w)
            ;;=> i is less than w, our element must be in that
            ;;    tree, we look in that one using lookup-tree.
                          (r8-lookup-tree w t i)
                          (recur ts*
```

```
                                    (- i w)))))
                     ;;=> i is greater than w, we must continue
                     ;;   searching for the tree containing it,
                     ;;   so we recur over the rest of trees.
```

8. Taking inspiration from `r8-lookup-tree` and `r8-lookup`, we can build `r8-update-tree` and `r8-update`:

```
(defn r8-update-tree
  [w ts index y]
  (match [w ts index]
         [1 a 0]  y
         ;;=> Analogous to look-up. we return
         ;;   a modified node with value y if
         ;;   we had a single node at index 0.
         [1 a i]  :index-error
         ;;=> Same as look-up, we are searching for
         ;;   and index greater than 0 for a single
         ;;   node tree. We raise an exception.
         [w [a t1 t2] 0] [y t1 t2]
         ;;=> Simplest case. We want to modify
         ;;   The root.
         [w [a t1 t2] i] (if (<= i (int (/ w 2)))
                           [ a
                             (r8-update-tree (int (/ w 2))
                                             t1
                                             (dec i)
                                             y)
                           t2]
         ;;=> The element we want to update
         ;;   is situated in the sub-tree at right.
         ;;   recur over that part.
                           [a
                            t1
                            (r8-update-tree (int (/ w 2))
                                            t2
                                            (- i 1 (int (/ w 2)))
                                            y) ])))
         ;;=> The other direction,
         ;;   we recur over the sub-tree at left.
(defn r8-update
  [ts index y]
```

```
(match [ts index]
       [[] i] :index-error
       ;;=> we can't update an empty tree.
       [[[w t] & ts*] i] (if (< i w)
                          (into [[w (r8-update-tree w t i y)]]
ts*)
;;=> i is less than w, the element we are seeking must be in this
;;    tree, we launch update-tree in it.
                          (into [[w t]] (r8-update ts*
                                         (- i w)
                                         y))))))
                          ;; else, we continue seeking for
                          ;; the tree containing our index i,
                          ;; recurring over the rest of them.
```

9. We can now test our implementation. First, we'll construct a list of 6 elements. Type the following into your REPL:

```
(def six-elts  (->> [[1 :elt1]]
                    (r8-cons :elt2)
                    (r8-cons :elt3)
                    (r8-cons :elt4)
                    (r8-cons :etl5)
                    (r8-cons :elt6)))
```

10. The `six-elts` function evaluates to:

```
[[3 [:elt6 :etl5 :elt4]] [3 [:elt3 :elt2 :elt1]]]
```

11. Two trees of 3 elements each, `:elt6` being the first element-remember that `consing` adds at the head. Let's access the lists's head:

```
(r8-head six-elts)
;; => :elt6
```

12. Let's now access the list's tail:

```
(r8-tail six-elts)
;; => [[1 :etl5] [1 :elt4] [3 [:elt3 :elt2 :elt1]]]
```

13. This leads us to 3 trees: the two one-element trees that were tied to the head and one other three-element tree. Let's consider one more element to `six-elts` and see what happens:

```
(r8-cons :elt7 six-elts)
  [[7 [:elt7 [:elt6 :etl5 :elt4] [:elt3 :elt2 :elt1]]]]
```

14. Neat. This has turned into 1 tree of exactly 7 elements. The rules of incrementing with the use of weights is applied here. Let's now show the second element of `six-elts`:

```
(r8-lookup six-elts 1)
;; => :etl5
```

15. This turns out to be the element that comes just after `:elt6`. Finally, let's update that second element:

```
(r8-update six-elts 1 :elt5-changed)
;; => [[3 [:elt6 :elt5-changed :elt4]] [3 [:elt3 :elt2 :elt1]]]
```

3
Walking Down Forests of Data

In this chapter, we will focus on trees. We will cover the following recipes:

- ▶ Building self-balancing and search-efficient splay trees
- ▶ Designing an efficient key-value store using B-trees
- ▶ Devising an undo-capable data structure using a rope
- ▶ Designing an autocomplete system using a trie

Introduction

In this chapter, we'll delve into some particular types of trees. As you will see through the recipes, using one or the other of these data-structures is motivated by the urge to address some very specific problematic while exposing an interesting algorithmic solution to the case being studied. For instance, we'll see some tree data structures that try to address efficiency of elements' access, along with others that are used as powerful tool empowering us to with advanced string manipulation capabilities. In this chapter, we'll cover the following recipes:

- ▶ **Building self-balancing, search-efficient splay trees**: This data structure is an enhancement to the binary search trees, providing for a mechanism to keep a good balance among the trees elements, while permitting a more efficient access to its most accessed elements.

- ▸ **B-trees**: B-trees are commonly used in databases and filesystems, thus we will design a B-tree in order to implement a minimalistic key-value store. A B-tree is a tree data structure whose nodes can refer to more than two children (as in binary search trees) and as such, are very well-suited for block-oriented systems.

- ▸ **Rope**: A rope is an interesting alternative to arrays as far as strings are concerned. As a special case of binary search trees, it allows you to traverse your strings very efficiently. Even if it gains significant size, reading characters at random indices beneath this string still runs at an amortized worst case O(log n). In addition to this, ropes are inherently persistent, that is, updating them is not destructive. Hence, they provide for a very elegant solution to fuel text editors for instance, as they are able to handle very large text while permitting very efficient undo capability.

- ▸ **Trie**: This tree data structure allows us to store prefixed data. You can think of a prefix as a means to store a set of strings so to efficiently determine all the elements that begin with any given set of characters. Tries are used to provide the functionality of word auto-completion in text editors, for instance.

Building self-balancing, search-efficient splay trees

One widely used tree structure for storing data are binary search trees. For instance, in order to store an element into such trees, you'd recursively walk it down, seeing every time how the value you're inserting compares in regard to the one stored in the node currently being visited if it is less you carry-on with the same process visiting the left sub-tree, else you'd dive into the right branch. Searching pretty much follows the same logic, recursively descending the tree and deciding at each level if you'd go left or right.

Now the most common problem with these trees is balance, or the lack thereof if left uncontrolled, one branch of the binary search tree could get substantially longer than the other, leading to inefficient access times.

Self-balancing binary search trees were devised to address this matter. These trees have the capability to rearrange themselves on insert operations, so their left and right branches' depth are kept pretty close. Splay trees fall in this category, but they show, in addition to this, one more interesting property. The accessed elements are moved to the top of a splay tree, making these kind of trees capable of somehow caching the most frequently accessed values near the top, thus speeding up access to most frequently accessed elements.

 Splay trees whose elements are strictly accessed in a nondecreasing order can become very close to a linear structure, thus breaking the promise of the balance they were supposed to offer. However, an amortized analysis of their behavior shows that they still offer an advantageous *O(log n)*.

To insert or access an element, we first perform these operations as in a normal binary search tree. Then, we perform splaying, that is, we move the accessed or inserted element to the top and proceed with one of the following three steps until the element is at the root of the tree:

1. **The zig step**: This step is carried out when the parent (which we'll call as **p**) of the inserted or accessed node (which we'll label as **x**) is at the root of the tree. The tree is then rotated on its edge between **p** and **x**. This is shown in the following figure. Note that though we present a case where **x** is to the left, the same step must be followed when **x** is to the right. The following figure shows the splay tree zig:

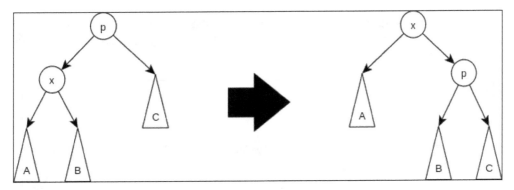

Splay tree zig by Zig.gif: User:Regnaronderivative work

 More information on "Splay tree zig " can be found at http://commons.wikimedia.org/wiki/File:Splay_tree_zig.svg#/media/File:Splay_tree_zig.svg.

2. **The zig-zig step**: This step is followed when **p** is not at the root and **p** and **x** are aligned to the left or right, as shown in the next figure. Here, they only portray the left case, but the right case can easily be deduced as well:

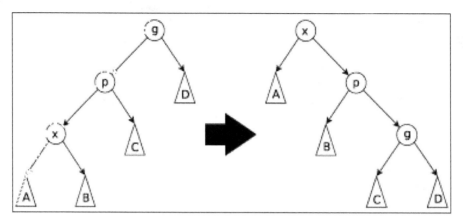

The zig-zig step

 More information on the zig zig step can be found at `http://commons.wikimedia.org/wiki/File:Zigzig.gif#/media/File:Zigzig.gif`.

3. **The zig-zag step**: This is done where **p** is not at the root and **p** and **x** are on different sides of the tree, as shown in the next figure. Here it only portrays **p** to the right and **x** as its left child:

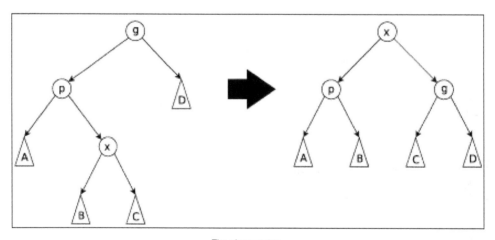

The zig-zag step

More information on the zig-zag step can be found at `http://commons.wikimedia.org/wiki/File:Zigzag.gif#/media/File:Zigzag.gif`.

How to do it...

1. First of all, as we'll use `core.match`, let's declare our `ns` (namespace) accordingly:

```
(ns recipe9.core
  (:require [clojure.core.match :refer [match]]))
```

2. Now, we'll begin by the two zig steps, to the right and left, using `core.match` to generate our trees according to their structures and to generate the structures that we seek:

```
(defn zig-right
  [tree]
  (match [tree] [{:node p
                  ;; p is at root
                  :left {:node x :left x-tr-left
                          :right x-tr-right}
                  ;; x is at left
                  :right p-tr-right }]  {:node x
                                         :left x-tr-left
                                         :right {:node p
                                                 :left x-tr-right
                                                 :right p-tr-right}}
      ;; If not matching this structure, we leave the tree as is
                  :else tree))

(defn zig-left
  [tree]
  (match [tree] [{:node p
                  ;; p is at root
                  :left p-tr-left
                  :right {:node x
                          ;; x is at right
                          :left x-tr-left
                          :right x-tr-right}}] {:node x
                                                :left {:node p
```

```
                                                :left p-tr-left
                                               :right x-tr-left}
                                           :right x-tr-right}
;; If not matching the structure, we return the same tree
                          :else tree))
```

3. Then, we'll implement functions for the zig-zig step, to the right and left versions:

```
(defn zig-zig-right
  [tree]
  (match [tree]
         [{:node g
           :left {:node p
                  :left {:node x}}}] (-> tree
                                          zig-right
                                          zig-right)
         :else tree))

(defn zig-zig-left
  [tree]
  (match [tree]
         [{:node g
           :right {:node p
                   :right {:node x}}}] (-> tree
                                            zig-left
                                            zig-left)
         :else tree))
```

4. Now, we'll focus on the zig-zag step, where x is to the right or to the left:

```
(defn zig-zag-left
  [tree]
  (match [tree] [{:node g
                  :left {:node p
                         :right {:node x}}
                  :right g-right}]   (->> (:left tree)
                                           zig-left
                                           (assoc {:node g
                                                   :right g-right}
                                                  :left)
                                           zig-right)
                 :else tree))
```

```
(defn zig-zag-right
  [tree]
  (match [tree]
        [{:node g
          :right {:node p
                  :left {:node x}}
          :left g-left}] (->> (:right tree)
                              zig-right
                              (assoc {:node g
                                       :left g-left}
                                     :right)
                              zig-left)
        :else tree))
```

5. Let's define `seek-or-insert`, which is a function that'll traverse or update our splay in a binary search tree. If the element is not found, it is inserted in the tree. This function returns a map containing the tree (it is updated if x is not found) and a path referring to x, which is a vector you can use with `get-in`, for instance:

```
(defn seek-or-insert
  [tree x]
  (if (empty? tree)
    {:new-tree {:node x :left nil :right nil} :new-path []}
;;=> If tree is empty we return one with x as its only element
    (loop [subtree tree
           path []]
      (if (nil? subtree)
        {:new-tree (assoc-in tree path {:node x
                                         :left nil
                                         :right nil})
         :new-path path}
;;=> end of the recursion, we return the tree and the path
        (cond (< x (get subtree :node)) (recur (get subtree :left)
                                               (conj path :left))
;;=> else if x is less than node, we recur left
              (> x (get subtree :node)) (recur (get subtree
:right)
                                               (conj path :right))
;;=> or we recur right
              (= x (get subtree :node)) {:new-tree tree
;;=> or we return x as we found it
                                         :new-path path}))))))
```

6. As we'll prepend the modification walking upward in the tree, we'll need some functions to get to the parents and grandparents of a given path. Remember that a path is a vector that permits a function such as get-in to attain an element in a nested structure. Hence, an element's parent is its path minus the last element and its grandparent is its path minus the two last elements:

```
(defn parent-path
  [path]
  (pop path))

(defn parent
  [tree path]
  (if (empty? path)
    nil
    (get-in tree (parent-path path))))

(defn grand-parent-path
  [path]
  (-> path pop pop))

(defn grand-parent
  [tree path]
  (if (or  (empty? path)
           (empty? (pop path)))
    nil
    (get-in tree (grand-parent-path path))))
```

7. Now, we will define our splay function. It uses a convenience function, put-transformed-in-tree, that updates a tree on a particular path with the result of the application of an arbitrary function to another tree. The splay function applies the steps that we've saw before according to its parameter structure and returns a splayed tree along with the information about whether the tree needs further splaying or not, so it can be used in a recursive way:

```
(defn put-transformed-in-tree
  [tree path fn-transform subtree]
  (let [transf  (fn-transform subtree)]
    (if (empty? path)
      transf
      (assoc-in tree path transf))))
(defn splay
  [tree path]
  (let [x (get-in tree path)
```

```
          p (if (empty? path)
               nil
               (parent tree path))
          g (if (nil? parent)
               nil
               (grand-parent tree path))]
;;=> Getting parent and grand parents
     (if (not (nil? p))
       (if (nil? g)
         (match [p]
               [{:left x}] {:spl-tree  (zig-right p)
                            :end true}
               [{:right x}] {:spl-tree  (zig-left p)
                             :end true})
;;=> applying zigs right or left. this step is considered final
         (let [gpath (grand-parent-path path)]
           (match [g]
               [{:left  {:left x}}] {:spl-tree
                                 (put-transformed-in-tree tree
gpath
zig-zig-right

                                                                 g)
                                 :end false}
               [{:right {:right x}}] {:spl-tree
                                 (put-transformed-in-tree tree
gpath
zig-zig-left

                                                                 g)
                                 :end false}
               ;;=> Applying zig-zigs left and right. Not final,
               ;;    we may go up in the tree
               [{:left {:right x}}] {:spl-tree
                                 (put-transformed-in-tree tree
gpath
zig-zag-left

                                                                 g)
                                 :end false}
               [{:right {:left x}}] {:spl-tree
                                 (put-transformed-in-tree tree
gpath
zig-zag-right

                                                                 g)
:end false}))))
```

```
;;=> Applying zig-zags left and right. Not final,
;;    we may go up in the tree
      {:spl-tree  tree :end true})))
;;    no parent, x is at root, we consider this step final
```

8. Finally, let's write or seek and insert the main function that will recursively call `splay` in order to construct our splay tree:

```
(defn insert-or-seek-into-splay-tree
  [tree x]
  (let [seek-or-insert-op (seek-or-insert tree x)]
    ;;=> We insert or find x,
    (loop [tree-before-splay (seek-or-insert-op :new-tree)
           path (seek-or-insert-op :new-path)]
    ;;=> And get the new tree and the path to get to it
    ;;    And begin our recursion
      (let [splay-op (splay tree-before-splay path)
            spl-tree (splay-op :spl-tree)
            end? (splay-op :end)]
      ;;=> We splay, getting the new splayed tree version
      ;;    And the inforamation about whether we shall stop
        (if end?
          spl-tree
      ;;=> End of recursion, we return last splayed version
          (let [new-seek-op (seek-or-insert spl-tree x)
                new-path (new-seek-op :new-path)]
      ;;=> Or we recur over the new splayed version
      ;;    and the new place where x is
            (recur spl-tree new-path)))))))
```

9. Now, let's insert some elements in a splay tree and see how it behaves. Input the following in your REPL:

```
(-> {}
                  (insert-or-seek-into-splay-tree 1)
                  (insert-or-seek-into-splay-tree 5)
                  (insert-or-seek-into-splay-tree 3)
                  (insert-or-seek-into-splay-tree 4)
                  (insert-or-seek-into-splay-tree 2)
                  (insert-or-seek-into-splay-tree 1))
```

10. Here's the structure that you'll get after completing the preceding step:

```
{:node 1,
 :right
```

```
{:node 2,
 :right
 {:node 4,
  :right {:node 5, :right nil, :left nil},
  :left {:node 3, :right nil, :left nil}},
 :left nil},
:left nil}
```

Note that 1 is at top of the tree followed by 2, 4, and so on. The most recently accessed items are near the top. The elements 3 and 5 are put on the same level for balance, whereas the elements 1, 2, and 4 are quite linear due to the access sequence we've completed.

Designing an efficient key-value store using B-trees

B-trees are commonly used in databases and filesystems, thanks to their inherent capability of manipulating large blocks of data. In contrast to a classical binary search tree, a B-tree is a tree data structure whose nodes can refer to more than two children nodes, and as such, traversing it permits us to access efficient block-oriented data. Besides, B-trees are self-balanced and designed in such a way that they grow very gracefully.

B-tree nodes are commonly called as keys. This is to refer to the fact that they hold values that act as separators. Indeed, for each node holding one particular key value, we find to its left, children that hold the keys of inferior value and to its right, a set of children with superior values. Although the values that B-tree nodes hold are labeled as keys, they still are values and can, besides acting as separators, represent actual data.(These keys are not to be confused with the keys of the key-value datastore that we will build for our recipe).

The following figure shows how a B-tree looks like and this can be found at `http://commons.wikimedia.org/wiki/File:B-tree.svg#/media/File:B-tree.svg`.

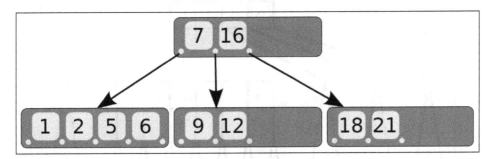

An example of a 3-5 B-Tree

To seek a value in a B-tree, you must recursively check between which two keys this value is situated and carry on with the process of visiting the set referred to by the children of interval of the found key. Say, you are looking for **3** and you have the keys **2** and **5**, then you'll have to look for your value in the right-hand side child of the key **2** (or in the left-hand side child of the key **5**). For convenience, we will only look at the right-hand side children of the keys, expect for the first one, whose left-hand side child holds all the values inferior to its own. When you reach a leaf node, the value you search for ought to be there; otherwise, it is not present in the B-tree. The following figure explains how we can access a value and the source can be found at `http://opendatastructures.org`.

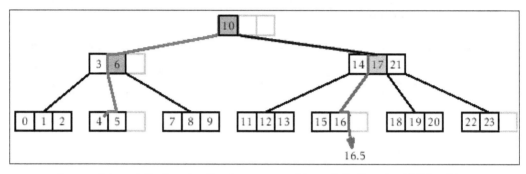

A successful search (for the value 4) and an unsuccessful search (for the value 16.5) in a B-tree

Insertion follows pretty much the same pattern; you recursively traverse your B-tree, the same process as explained for searching, until you reach a leave node, where you'd insert your value and make sure that the result set is sorted in the increasing order. However, there's a rule that you need to observe though. Nodes are not allowed to store more than a maximum number of keys. If this situation arises, when you insert your value, this node must be split in two and its median element must be migrated to the set of keys that are directly situated above. This is explained in the following figure, and the source can be found at `http://opendatastructures.org`.

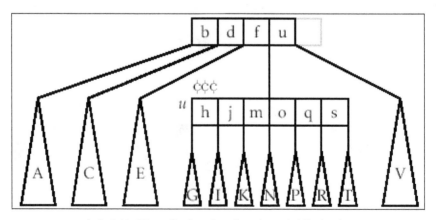

An instable B-tree after insertion of an element at the level u

The figure that follows shows the migration of **m** to the preceding node, and the source can be found at `http://opendatastructures.org`.

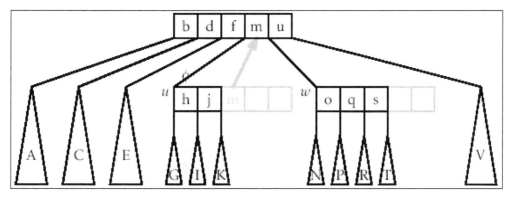

Splitting "u" and migrating m to the node

How to do it...

1. First, we are going to implement a function that given a node and key, returns the path. A vector makes it possible for us to access a nested structure and can be used by functions such as `get-in` of the interval that contains that key:

```
(defn where-to-insert-key-in-node
  [current-b-node a-key]
  (let [current-node-keys  (mapv :key current-b-node)
        first-key (first current-node-keys)
        last-key  (peek current-node-keys)
        key-intervals (into [] (partition 2
                                          1
                                          current-node-keys))]
;;=> first we get the first and last keys,
;;    then we construct the keys intervals
    (if (< a-key first-key)
      [0 :left]
;;=> we return the path to the elements before first key
      (if (> a-key last-key)
        [(dec (count current-node-keys)) :right]
;;=> we return the path to the elements after last key
        (let [the-interval (first  (filter #(and (> a-key (first %))
                                                 (< a-key (last %)))
                                      key-intervals))
              the-interval-pos (.indexOf key-intervals the-interval)]
;;=> else we return in which interval is our key situated
          [the-interval-pos :right])))))
```

```
;;=> and we return the path
;;    to the interval
```

2. Then, we must come up with a function that determines where to insert the key in a B-tree, using the function we developed in the preceding code:

```
(defn where-to-insert-key-in-b-tree
  [btree a-key]
  (loop [path []
         stree btree]
    (if (empty? (get (first  stree) :right))
      path
;;=> if no more children, we return the path of that leaf.
      (let [path-in-stree (where-to-insert-key-in-node stree a-key)
            new-path (into path path-in-stree)]
        (recur new-path
               (get-in stree new-path))))))
;;=> else we recur with the path found by the function
;;    where-to-insert-key-in-node, and the tree pointed
;;    by that function
```

3. Now, we are going to build `verif-tree`, which verifies a node in a path, and whenever it finds that it has violated the maximum elements rule, it migrates the median to the node above the current node pointed out by this path. It also recursively does this job to make sure that the act of handing over of the median to an upper node doesn't cause it to violate the maximum elements rule.

 Note that in the code, we always make sure that our key sets are sorted in the increasing order.

4. This functions uses `grand-parent`, whose implementation is given in the following code snippet:

```
(defn grand-parent-path
  [path]
  (if (and (not (empty? path))
           (not (empty? (pop path))))
    (-> path pop pop)
    []))

(defn verif-tree
  [b-tree
   path
   max-elts]
  (let [v-to-verif (into [] (sort-by :key
```

```
                                        <
                                (get-in b-tree path))))]
        (if (< (count v-to-verif)
              max-elts)
          b-tree ;;=> we are not violating max elements rule,
                  ;;   we leave the tree as-is.
          (let [gpath (grand-parent-path path)
                median (int (/ (count v-to-verif )
                               2))
                new-left (->>
                            (subvec v-to-verif
                                    0
                                    median)
                            (sort-by :key <)
                            (into []))

                new-right (->>  (subvec v-to-verif (inc median))
                                (sort-by :key <)
                                (into []))

                new-key  (get v-to-verif median)
                ;;=> else we compute the first and second halves
                ;;   and the key to be migrated.
                new-b-tree-in-path (if (not (empty? path))
                                    (assoc-in b-tree
                                              path
                                              new-left)
                                    new-left)]
        ;;=>  The node to contain the first half of what it used to have
            (if (not (empty? gpath))
              (recur  (update-in new-b-tree-in-path
                          ;;=> we recursively update our tree
                          ;;   to be sure that our migrating key
                          ;;   does not violate maximum elements rule
                          ;;   in the node it has landed in.
                              gpath
                              (comp (partial into [])
                                    (partial sort-by :key <)
                                    conj)
                              ;;=> we make sure our key sets are
                              ;;   sorted in increasing order
                              (assoc new-key
                                    :right
                                    new-right
```

```
                                        :left new-left))
                    gpath
                    max-elts)
;;=> If grand-parent is not empty,
;;    we update it adding the new key pointing to the second half
            [(-> new-key
          (assoc :right new-right :left  new-b-tree-in-path))])))))
              ;;=> Else, we must be at a root node, we simply
              ;;    set it to a new tree containing the key pointing
              ;;    to the second half
```

5. Now, we will develop `insert-in-b-tree`. We will begin by inserting the key where it initially belongs, yield an instable tree, and then we will run `verif-tree` on it so that it can transform it into a proper B-tree, splitting the nodes that violate the maximum elements rule if needed:

```
(defn insert-in-b-tree
  [max-elts b-tree a-key a-val]
  (let [path-insert (where-to-insert-key-in-b-tree b-tree a-key)
        instable-new-tree     (if (empty? path-insert)
                                (into [] (sort-by :key
                                                  <
                                                  (conj b-tree
                                                    {:key a-key
                                                     :val a-val
                                                   :right [] :left []})))
                                (update-in b-tree
                                           path-insert
                                           (comp (partial into [])
                                           (partial sort-by :key <)
                                                 conj)
                                           {:key a-key
                                            :val a-val
                                            :right []
                                            :left []})))]
    ;;=> we construct an instable B-Tree, that is, one that
    ;;    maybe causes the node it is in to exceed the maximum
    ;;    allowed elements.
    (verif-tree instable-new-tree
                path-insert
                max-elts)))
    ;;=> verif-tree executes to recursively split the nodes above
    ;;    if needed.
```

6. Finally, we can implement `seek-in-b-tree`, which given a key, tells us which value it stores. This is the very function that provides the key-value datastore functionality that we initially wanted:

```
(defn seek-in-b-tree
  [b-tree a-key]
  (let [node-is-here (first (filter #(= (:key  %) a-key)
                                    b-tree ))]
    (if (not (nil? node-is-here))
      (:val node-is-here)
      ;; =>if key is found in this node, we return the value
      ;;    it holds.
      (let [node-keys (mapv :key b-tree)
            first-key (first node-keys)
            last-key (peek node-keys)
            key-intervals (partition 2 1 node-keys)
            next-s-tree-path (if (<  a-key first-key)
                               [0 :left]
                               (if (> a-key last-key )
                                 [(dec (count node-keys)) :right ]
            (let [the-interval (first (filter #(and (a-key > (first %))
                                                    (a-key < (last %)))
                                              key-intervals))
                  pos-interval (.indexOf key-intervals the-interval)]
              [pos-interval :right])))
            next-s-tree (get-in b-tree next-s-tree-path)]
        ;;=> else, we find which interval to look in,
        ;;   and get to this next-s-tree in a recur
        (if (empty? next-s-tree)
          nil
          ;;=> if nex-s-tree is empty, end of recursion, key is not present
          (recur next-s-tree a-key))))))
        ;;=> else we still recur over next-s-tree
```

7. Let's insert some values in our datastore and see how it behaves. First, we will create a convenience function so that we don't have to specify the max elements for each call:

```
(def insert-in-b-tree-3 (partial insert-in-b-tree 3))
```

How it works...

1. We insert some values in our key-value datastore:

```
(def btree   (-> []
                                        (insert-in-b-tree-3 0 "a")
                                        (insert-in-b-tree-3 1 "b")
                                        (insert-in-b-tree-3 2 "c")
                                        (insert-in-b-tree-3 5 "d")
                                        (insert-in-b-tree-3 4 "e")
                                        (insert-in-b-tree-3 3 "g")))
```

2. The resulting `btree` function is the value that we pass along with `key 4`:

```
[{:key 4,
  :val "e",
  :right [{:key 5, :val "d", :right [], :left []}],
  :left
  [{:key 1,
    :val "b",
    :right
    [{:key 2, :val "c", :right [], :left []}
     {:key 3, :val "g", :right [], :left []}],
    :left [{:key 0, :val "a", :right [], :left []}]}]}]
Let's see the value of key 6:
(seek-in-b-tree btree 6)
;; => nil
Quite natural, we have no element with key 6.
Let's see the value of key 4:
(seek-in-b-tree btree 4)
;; => "e"
```

Devising an undo-capable data structure using a rope

Traditionally, a string is represented using an array of characters. To access it, you would have to sequentially traverse it, which is far from efficient, especially if the string gets long. Besides, such implementation relies on a mutable state; any update on the strings that are implemented as char arrays will necessarily destroy any older versions of them. This will leave us with no option, but to maintain the history through inefficient copying if we need to track the different versions of a particular long string, as text editors do, for instance.

A rope is an interesting alternative to character arrays as far as string representation is concerned. In addition to this, ropes are inherently persistent, that is, updating them is not destructive and stands as a very elegant solution for text editors, for instance, as they are able to handle very large texts and are able to still permit undo capability very easily. A rope is a binary search tree whose leaves hold short portions of text. At every internal node, we store the number of characters represented by its left-hand side children. So, finding a string is a matter of recursively descending that binary search tree, deciding at each level to go left if the index is less than the value stored in the visited element, or to go right otherwise. The following figure shows a sample rope:

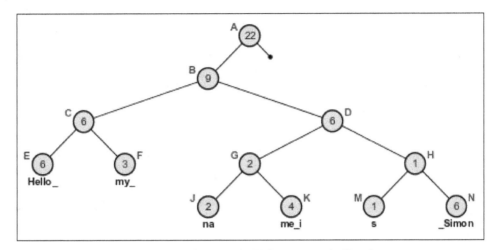

A sample rope for the string "Helle_my_name_is_Simon"

The source can be found at http://en.wikipedia.org/wiki/File:Rope_example.jpg.

For media, visit http://commons.wikimedia.org/wiki/File:Vector_Rope_example.svg#/media/File:Vector_Rope_example.svg.

The internal nodes are called **concat** nodes, whereas the leaves are labeled as **short nodes**. A concat node may contain two children that may be combinations of a concat or short node.

We are going to focus on the following operations of ropes:

▶ **Concat**: In this, when we have two ropes, we concatenate them into a single new rope. When we concatenate two ropes, a new concat node is created, and we must compute the length of the string represented by its left-hand side child. The two rules for two special cases are given here, so that the tree is balanced pretty well:

  ❑ Two short nodes concatenate into a flat tree whose root is a concat node and whose leaves are the initial short nodes

  ❑ A left-hand side rope with a right-hand side child holding a short node and a right-hand side rope consisting only a short node concatenate a rope which concatenates the first rope's left-hand side son and the two leaves.

A sample concat operation is shown in the following figure, and the source can be found at `https://commons.wikimedia.org/wiki/File:Vector_Rope_concat.svg#/media/File:Vector_Rope_concat.svg`.

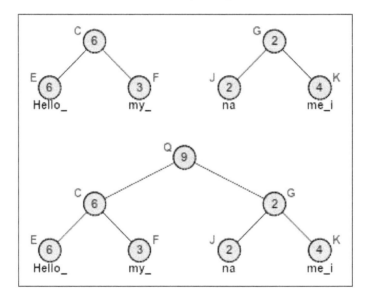

Vector Rope concat

▶ **Splitting**: This operation is about splitting two ropes in an index. If the splitting occurs exactly at the beginning of a short node, all the right links that occur after the index are broken, yielding two new ropes: one containing the short nodes that were left to the index (while recomputing values for all the concat nodes present in this first part) and one containing the nodes which were to the right. If the split occurs in the middle of a short, we replace it by two shorts that are split at the index and proceed as if we were splitting at the beginning of a short node we did in the first case. A sample splitting operation is shown in the following figure, and the source can be found at `http://commons.wikimedia.org/wiki/File:Vector_Rope_split.svg#/media/File:Vector_Rope_split.svg`.

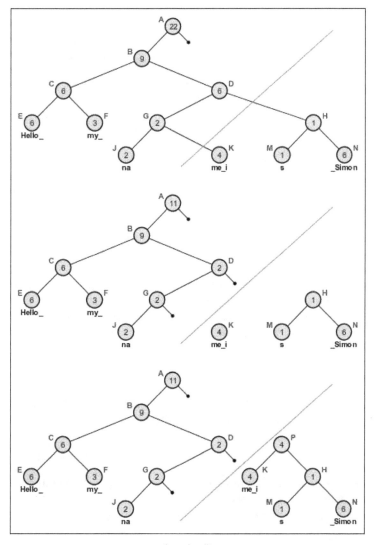

A rope split

- **Getting a character at index**: Here, we get the character that is stored in the given index. This is pretty much like a binary search tree traversal, that is, if the index if less than the value stored in the current concat node, we descend to the left; otherwise, we descend to the right and search with a new index, that is, the old index minus the value that was stored in the concat node.

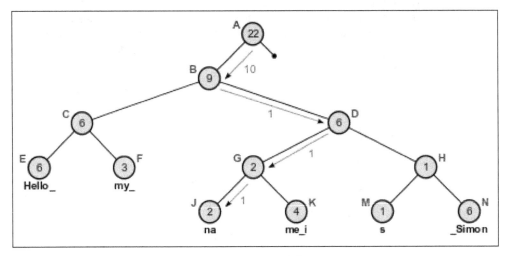

Accessing a rope at index

 The source can be found at `http://commons.wikimedia.org/wiki/File:Vector_Rope_index.svg#/media/File:Vector_Rope_index.svg`.

- **Deleting from a source index to a target index**: This can be done by two splits and a concat, that is, we first split the rope at the destination index, than we split the right resulting rope at the target index minus the source index, and then we concat the first rope and the right-hand side rope resulting from the second split.

How to do it...

1. First of all, as we are going to make use of `core.match`; let's declare our ns (namespace), so that we can import that library:

    ```
    (ns recipe11.core
            (:require [clojure.core.match :refer [match]]))
    ```

2. Now, we'll define `concat-ropes` function. This is quite a long function, but if you follow through, you should recognize all the cases we are using with `core.match` that occur when we concatenate two ropes:

    ```
    (defn concat-ropes
    ```

```
[rope1 rope2]
(match [rope1 rope2]
       [[] r2] r2
       [r1 []] r1
       [nil r] r
       [r nil] r
       [{:short left-s-str}
        {:short short-str} ] [{:concat (count left-s-str)}
                                     [{:short left-s-str}
                                      {:short short-str}]]
       [[{:concat _}
         [(([{:concat len-left-c}
            [s-s-left [{:concat s-s-right-1} _]]] :as left-son)
          {:short right-son}]]
         {:short short-str} ] [{:concat
                                (+ len-left-c s-s-right-1)}
                               [left-son
                                [{:concat (count right-son)}
                                 [{:short right-son}
                                  {:short short-str}]]]]]
        [[{:concat _}
          [(([{:concat len-left-c}
             [s-s-left {:short s-right} ]] :as left-son)
           {:short right-son}]]
          {:short short-str}] [{:concat
                               (+ len-left-c
                                  (count s-right))}
                            [left-son [{:concat (count right-son)}
                                       [{:short right-son}
                                        {:short short-str}]]]]]
        [[{:concat rope-len}
          [left-son
           [{:concat len-r-c } _]]]
          {:short short-str} ] [{:concat (+ rope-len len-r-c)}
                                [rope1 {:short  short-str}]]
       [[{:concat rope-len} [{:short l-son}
                             {:short r-son}]]
        {:short short-str} ] [{:concat (+ rope-len
                                          (count r-son))}
                              [rope1 {:short short-str}]]
       [[{:concat len1}
         [_ [{:concat len2 } _]]] _] [{:concat (+ len1 len2)}
                                      [rope1 rope2]]
       [[{:concat len1}
```

```
            [_ {:short str2}]] _] [{:concat (+ len1 (count str2))}
                                        [rope1 rope2]]
        [{:short str} _] [{:concat (count str)}
                        [rope1 rope2]]
        [[{:concat l1} _] [{:concat _} [_ [{:concat l2} _ ]]]]
[{:concat (+  l1 l2)} [rope1 rope2]]
        [[{:concat l1} _] [{:concat _} [_ {:short s2}]]]
[{:concat (+  l1 (count s2))} [rope1 rope2]]))
```

3. Now, we will develop `get-rope-at-index`:

```
(defn get-from-rope-at-index
  [rope index]
  (loop [current-rope rope
         current-index index
         path []]
    (let [current-node (if (vector? current-rope)
                          (first current-rope )
                          current-rope)]
      ;;=> We are representing our ropes as vectors
      ;;   of vectors, and at times we may find shorts
      ;;   that are maps. hence, the test above.
      (if (not (nil? (get  current-node :concat)))
      ;;=> we are at a concat node
        (if (< (get current-node :concat)  current-index )
          (recur (get  (second current-rope) 1)
                 (- current-index  (:concat current-node))
                 (conj path 1 1))
      ;;=> We recur right, index > concat val
          (recur (get (second current-rope) 0 )
                 current-index
                 (conj path 1 0)))
      ;;=> We recur left,
        (let [current-str (:short  current-node )
              max-idx ( count current-str)]
          (if (and  (<=  current-index max-idx)
                    (>=  current-index 1))
      ;;=> if index in interval
            {:char (str (nth  current-str (dec  current-index)))
             :short current-str
             :path path
             :idx-in-str  (dec  current-index)}
      ;;=> we return a map containing all the information
            nil))))))

;;   else we return nil
```

4. Now, we'll focus on how to split the rope. The final output of this operation will be two ropes: a left rope containing the nodes that we keep and a right rope that will be the concatenation of the nodes we untied. First, we detect whether our index falls in the middle of a short and if so, we replace it with the concatenation of the two substrings result of splitting the initial rope at that very index. Then, we go from the path leading to the element situated at the index that we want to split and walk the tree up, untying every right sibling of a node whose parent is a left child. Finally, starting from the `short` rope kept at the right-hand side rope (that is, the right-hand side string before the index where we split), we go up the tree again, updating the values at the `concat` nodes and removing from each grandparent, the length of the string we removed. For this complex function, we define some helper routines that permit us to go up a rope, get a rope's parent path, or untie some node's right-hand side child:

```
(defn parent-path
  [path]
  ;;=> returns the path to this
  ;;    path's parent.
  (if (empty? path)
    nil
    (if (empty? (pop path))
        nil
        (-> path pop pop)))))

(defn unlink-right-child
  [rope]
  ;;=> returns the node without
  ;;    its right child.
  (let [parent (get rope 0)
        children (get rope 1)]
    [parent (pop children)]))

(defn right-child
  [rope]
  ;;=> returns the right child of a node
  (peek  (get rope 1)))

(defn is-left-child?
  [path]
  ;;=> returns whether this is
  ;;    the left child of his parent
  (if (empty? path)
    false
    (= (peek path) 0)))
```

```
(defn unlink-all-parents-right-children
  [rope from-path]
  (loop [left-rope rope
         right-rope []
         path from-path]
    (if path
      (let [p-path (parent-path path)]
        (recur   (if (is-left-child? path)
;;=> if we are at a left child
                   (if (not (empty? p-path))
                     (update-in left-rope p-path unlink-right-child)
                     (unlink-right-child  left-rope))
;;=> we untie the parent's right child
                   left-rope)
;;=> else we leave the rope as-is
                 (if (is-left-child? path)
                   ;;=> if we are at a left child
                   ;;   we add the removed right child
                   ;;   to the right rope
                   (concat-ropes right-rope
                                 (right-child (get-in left-rope
                                                      p-path)))
                   right-rope)
                 p-path))
;;=> and we recur going up in the tree
      [left-rope right-rope])))

(defn grand-parent-path
  [path]
  ;;=> returns the path to the current
  ;;   node grandparent
  (if-let [ppath (parent-path path)]
    (if-let [gpath (parent-path ppath)]
      gpath
      nil)
    nil))

(defn remove-from-all-gparents
  [rope from-path to-remove]
  ;;=> removes a quantity from all
  ;;   grand-parent, then grand-parent of grand-parent
  ;;   etc of from-path
  (loop [result-rope rope
         path from-path]
```

```
    (if-let [gpath (grand-parent-path path)]
      (let [rope-at-gpath (get-in result-rope gpath)]
        (recur (assoc-in result-rope (conj gpath 0 :concat)
                         (- (get (get rope-at-gpath 0) :concat)
                            to-remove))
               gpath))
      result-rope)))

(defn split-rope-at-index[rope index]
(let [{:keys [short path idx-in-str]}
(get-from-rope-at-index rope index)
        modified-rope (if (= idx-in-str (dec (count short)))
                        rope
                        (let [short-left (subs short 0
                                               (inc idx-in-str))
                              short-right (subs short
                                                (inc idx-in-str))]
                          (assoc-in rope
                                    path
                                    (concat-ropes {:short short-left}
                                                  {:short short-right}))))
    ;;=> first, if index falls in the middle of a short,
    ;;    we replace it by a concat of two new shorts :
    ;;    one for each part before and after the index.
    modified-path ( get (get-from-rope-at-index modified-rope
                                                index)
                        :path)
      ;;=> we get the path  we are going to start from
      ;;    in the modified rope
      tb-removed-from-gparents (- (count short) idx-in-str)
      ;;=> we prepare the quantity which will be removed
      ;;    from grand-parents
      [left-tr right-tr] (unlink-all-parents-right-children
                            ;;=> we proceed with the untying
                            modified-rope modified-path)]
  [(remove-from-all-gparents
    left-tr
    (conj  (pop modified-path) 0)
    tb-removed-from-gparents )
   ;;=> and then update the concats going up
   ;;    in the tree
   right-tr]))
```

5. Finally, as an application for the split and concat operation we devised, here are the `insert-into-rope-at-index` and `delete-from-rope-at-index` functions, which are self-explanatory:

```
(defn insert-into-rope-at-index
  [rope
   index
   short]
  (let [[rleft rright] (split-rope-at-index rope index)]
    (-> (concat rleft
                {:short short})
        (concat rright))))
```

```
(defn delete-from-rope-at-index
  [rope
   index-from
   index-to]
  (let [[rleft temp-rright] (split-rope-at-index rope
                                                 index-from)
        [rdeleted rright] (split-rope-at-index temp-rright
                                               (- index-to index-from))]
    {:new-rope (concat-ropes rleft
                             rright)
     :deleted-rope rdeleted}))
```

6. Let's see our rope in action now. We'll first have to construct a rope:

```
recipe11.core> (def rp   (-> []
                             (concat-ropes {:short "John"})
                             (concat-ropes {:short "is"})
                             (concat-ropes {:short "here"})
                             (concat-ropes {:short "with"})
                             (concat-ropes {:short "you"})))
```

7. The `rp` rope is structured as:

```
[{:concat 10}
 [[{:concat 6}
   [[{:concat 4} [{:short "John"} {:short "is"}]]
    [{:concat 4} [{:short "here"} {:short "with"}]]]]
  {:short "you"}]]
```

8. Now, let's split the rope at the position 5 (positions start from 1):

```
(split-rope-at-index rp 5)
```

9. You'll get the following output after this:

```
[[{:concat 8}
  [[{:concat 6}
     [[{:concat 2} [{:short "John"} [{:concat 1} [{:short
"i"}]]]]]]]]
  [{:concat 5}
   [[{:concat 1}
      [{:short "s"} [{:concat 4} [{:short "here"} {:short
"with"}]]]]]
     {:short "you"}]]]
```

10. Let's insert "ny" so that "John" becomes "Johnny":

```
(insert-into-rope-at-index rp 4 "ny")
```

11. Now, our rope looks like:

```
({:concat 10}
 [[{:concat 5} [[{:concat 4} [{:short "John"}]]]]]]
 [:short "ny"]
 {:concat 6}
 [[{:concat 2}
    [{:short "is"} [{:concat 4} [{:short "here"} {:short
"with"}]]]]
   {:short "you"}])
```

12. Finally, let's remove "here":

```
(delete-from-rope-at-index rp 6 10)
```

13. This generates the following output:

```
{:new-rope
 [{:concat 13}
  [[{:concat 10}
     [[{:concat 5} [[{:concat 4} [{:short "John"} {:short
"is"}]]]]]]]
    [{:concat 4} [{:short "with"} {:short "you"}]]]],
  :deleted-rope [{:concat 7} [[{:concat 4} [{:short "here"}]]]]}
```

Designing an autocomplete system using a trie

A trie is a particular tree data structure that makes it possible for us to store prefixed data. As you descend a trie, you construct prefixes. As such, a node's children share a common prefix, which is the one we constructed so far while descending the tree. In fact, tries are like automaton, where descending a branch is analogous to consuming a transition literal and the state you'd get into when you do so is the prefix of that target node.

Generally, nodes of a trie carry information about the transitions and can carry weight depending on their use.

One interesting application of tries is text autocompletion. You can store strings in a prefixed manner in a trie. These strings would span over the shared portions of the tree, which represent the part that is common to them and which are forked when they become different. An autocomplete system would then work by descending the tree as far as the text you'd feed it goes and then the system would carry on with the tree traversal, so that it can provide you with the strings that add to that initial radix you provided so possible completions are suggested. We'd store some weights in the nodes according to the number of times a particular state has been reached. Hence, we'll be able to sort our completion proposals, so that the most frequent words appear first. The following figure explains this process:

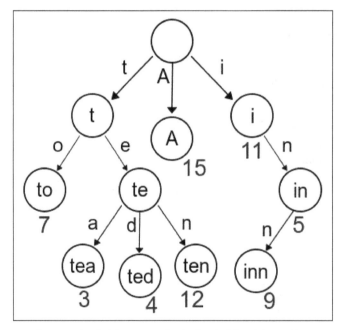

An example of a trie representing to, tea, ted, ten, I, in, and inn

The source can be found at `http://commons.wikimedia.org/` `wiki/File:Trie_example.svg#/media/File:Trie_example.` `svg`.

How to do it...

1. We begin by a function that inserts a string into a trie. We will use `merge-with`, and the key for our nodes will be the character of the word that is processed. As such, if the character is not present, it would be created with an `:nb` at `1`; otherwise, its effect will be to add 1 to the `:nb` of the entry referred by this character. At every step of the recursion, we add `:next` to the path, forcing the next character to be a son of the current level.

```
(defn insert-str-in-trie
  [trie the-string]
  (let [str-seq (map str the-string)]
    ;;=> we transform the string into a seq of
    ;;    chars.
    (loop [remaining-chars str-seq
           result trie
           path []]
      (if (seq remaining-chars)
        (let [path-in-node (conj path
                                 (first remaining-chars))]
          ;;=> we get the path to the node representing
          ;;    the state referred by this char in this
          ;;    level
          (recur (rest remaining-chars)
          ;;=>   we carry on with the rest of the chars
                 (update-in result
                            path-in-node
                            #(merge-with + % {:nb 1} ))
          ;; and   we update / insert a node referred by this char,
          ;; updating :nb, the number of times the sequence thus far
          ;; has appeared in our input
                 (conj path-in-node :next )))
          ;; => the path for descending is the value
          ;;     referred by :next key
        (update-in result (pop path) merge {:end true}))))))
        ;;=> end of recursion, we return the trie with
        ;;    an :end key set at true, to tell that this
        ;;    state represents a whole string
```

2. Next, we are going to implement `descend-branch`, which is able to process a single fork from a common radix (which is a shared string between two possible completion paths) and suggest a completion as soon as it meets a node whose `:end` key is true. Note that we emit a vector of maps, where each map contains a possible completion and the `:nb` amount to represent the number of times a completion has occurred:

```
(defn descend-branch
  [branch]
  (loop [cur-branch branch
         cur-result ""
         results []]
    (if (nil? cur-branch)
      results
      ;;=> end of recursion
      (let [c-key (if (vector? cur-branch)
                    ;; as we're applying this to
                    ;; map entries, we sometimes have to do
                    ;; with a vector [k v]
                    (get cur-branch 0)
                    ;; and sometimes with a map
                    (first (keys cur-branch)))]
;;=> This determines the key being processed for both cases
        (recur (if (vector? cur-branch )
                 (:next  (get cur-branch 1))
                 (get-in cur-branch [c-key :next]))
               ;;=> same logic, be it a vector or a map,
               ;;   we recur over the next element in
               ;;   the structure
               (str cur-result c-key)
               ;;=> we append the character to a current result buffer
               (let [new-cur-branch (if (vector? cur-branch)
                                      (get cur-branch 1 )
                                      (get cur-branch c-key))]
                 ;;=> next branch is also determined for both cases:
                 ;;   a vector or a map
                 (if (:end new-cur-branch)
;;=> if :end at true, i.e, this state represents a whole world
;;   we add current result buffer to the whole results vector
                   ;;   along with the number of times it occurred
                   (conj results {:result (str  cur-result c-key)
                                  :nb (get new-cur-branch :nb) })
                   results)))))))
```

3. Finally, we'll design our completions function. We have two portions to compute. Given the input upon which we have to suggest possible completions, we first have to find all the characters that are found in a straight path before they are forked. Then, we map `descend-branch` over the forks that we've found. Now, how can we determine whether the path has been forked? We can do so simply by recursively verifying that the count of elements contained in each node's map exceeds 1 to inform it that it has been forked. If it does, we stop and return the found portion as the completion of a shared path before forking. This portion is added to the path where we search for completions, and `descend-branch` carries on with the process. If we reach `nil`, that is, if the path never forks, we return an empty portion; we leave mapping of `descend-branch` and find all the alternatives, as this will give us the overlapping portions (as in John and Johnny completing for john). We do so because if we add the first phase computation related to a path of a branch that never forks, `descend-branch` will operate from the very end of the trie and hence will yield nothing. We must be sure that we add a path to our starting path only if it is related to a fork:

```
(defn completions
  [trie the-string]
  (let [str-seq (map str the-string)
        from-path (into []  (interleave str-seq (repeat :next) ))
;; => given an input string, we know that we'll
;;    start descending our tree from path [c1 :next c2 :next ...]
        rest-commons (loop [common-branch (get-in trie from-path )
                            r-commons []]
;;=> rest-commons is the result of phase 1 computation
                       (if (> (count common-branch) 1)
                         r-commons
;;=> we have reached a fork. the keys discovered
;;   so far can be added to the starting path computed out of
;;   input string.
                         (if  (nil? common-branch)
                           []
;;=> else we never forked. Thus far, we are at the
                           ;;    end of the trie. No forks were available,
                           ;;    so  we return nothing and we let
                           ;;    descend-branch compute all the overlapping
                           ;;    completions, as we are in a one strictly
                           ;;    sequential branch
                           (let [c-key (first (keys common-branch))]
                             (recur (get-in common-branch [c-key
:next])
                                    (conj r-commons c-key))))))))
;;=> else we recur building our r-commons vector
;;   descending the tree jumping :next by :next
```

```
                    rest-commons-path (interleave rest-commons (repeat :next))
                    ;;=> the path to add to begin with (if we found any forks)
                    str-commons (reduce str rest-commons)
                    ;;=> the string that lead to the forks if any.
                    possible-completions  (mapcat descend-branch
                                                   (get-in trie
                                                           (into from-path
                                                            rest-commons-path)))]
          ;;=> mapping descend branch over the branches
          ;;    determined by adding the path to the fork
          ;;    if any is present, or from the simple path
          ;;    computed out of the input string suffices as
          ;;    we are in a single way path.
          (if (not (empty? possible-completions))
             (into [] (map #(str the-string
                                 "|"
                                 str-commons
                                 (get % :result))
                        (sort-by :nb > possible-completions)))
             ;;=> We issue possible completions sorted by their
             ;;    frequency in the input
             [(str the-string "|"
                   str-commons)])))
     ;;=> descend-branch did not yield anything, we return
     ;;    the common-string as a completion (if we found any)
```

4. Now, we can observe our trie in action. We will start by creating trie:

```
(def tr  (-> {}
                          (insert-str-in-trie "john")
                          (insert-str-in-trie "john")
                          (insert-str-in-trie "johnny")
                          (insert-str-in-trie "joachim")
                          (insert-str-in-trie "is")
                          (insert-str-in-trie "isis")
                          (insert-str-in-trie "island")))
```

5. This is the structure of our trie:

```
{"i"
 {:next
  {"s"
   {:next
```

```
      {"l"
        {:next
          {"a"
            {:next {"n" {:next {"d" {:end true, :nb 1}}, :nb 1}}, :nb
1}},
          :nb 1},
         "i" {:next {"s" {:end true, :nb 1}}, :nb 1}},
        :end true,
        :nb 3}},
      :nb 3},
   "j"
   {:next
     {"o"
       {:next
         {"a"
           {:next
             {"c"
               {:next
                 {"h"
                   {:next {"i" {:next {"m" {:end true, :nb 1}}, :nb 1}}, :nb
1}},
                 :nb 1}},
             :nb 1},
           "h"
           {:next
             {"n"
               {:next {"n" {:next {"y" {:end true, :nb 1}}, :nb 1}},
                :end true,
                :nb 3}},
             :nb 3}},
         :nb 4}},
       :nb 4}}
```

6. Let's try some completions. Insert the following code in your REPL:

```
(completions tr "jo")
;; => ["jo|hn" "jo|achim" "jo|hnny"]
;"john" comes first as we inserted it twice
(completions tr "joh")
;; => ["joh|n" "joh|nny"]
```

4
Making Decisions with the Help of Science

In this chapter, we will cover those algorithms that assist in drawing educated conclusions from a few statements about various optimization or machine learning problems that we have provided. We will elaborate on the following recipes:

- ▶ Designing a live recommendation engine
- ▶ Resolving cost and profit optimization problems
- ▶ Finding an optimal path in a graph
- ▶ Summarizing text by extracting the most representative sentences

Introduction

We will address four types of problems that involve different kinds of decision making.

- ▶ **Designing a live recommendation engine**: Recommendation engines determine which items some users would most likely want to buy or visit a particular website for, given that we have some knowledge about their previous actions, as well as knowledge of all user behavior that was observed on an e-commerce website. We'll design such an engine based on the measurement of co-occurrence of events and lay down a data structure, making it possible for us to effectively process all user data as it flows through the system.

- ▶ **Resolving cost and profit optimization problems**: In this recipe, we will use an interesting technique that is widely used in artificial intelligence—branch and bound—in order to resolve a special case of optimization problems, where solutions can only be expressed as a linear combination of integer values. We'll apply this technique in the particular case of a bakery. We will decide how many pieces of each type of pastry must be made—given that there are some constraints on the cooking material to be used and we have some information about the selling prices—so that the profits of the bakery are maximized.

- ▶ **Finding an optimal path in a graph**: For this recipe, we will consider the problem of finding optimal paths using Dijkstra's algorithm. Given a graph description, that is, a set of weighted connections between given nodes, we will use this algorithm to find the optimal (shortest) path between a starting node and a target node.

- ▶ **Summarizing texts by extracting the most representative sentences**: Our last recipe focuses on the problem of text summarization and how it could be addressed using extractive methods, in which an original text is represented using a shorter set of its most salient sentences. Here, we will look, in particular, at the **LexRank algorithm** (inspired by Google's famous PageRank), which provides an elegant solution for this kind of approach to text summarization.

Designing a live recommendation engine

One widely used application of recommendation engines is to give an e-commerce site's visitor, as he/she performs various actions, such as clicking on products, buying goods, or performing searches, some relevant advice about items they have not visited yet but would be interested in. This way, e-commerce site owners increase the odds of purchases and drive more sales.

There are various ways of designing recommendation engines. In technical literature, we often find them classified in two great families. First, the engines that take into account the nature of the items being visited, that is, they use knowledge about the very products to recommend something - for instance, one would recommend batteries to a user who has bought a drummer bunny toy. These recommenders are labeled as **content based** and require specific knowledge about the products they deal with, and so, while providing a rather good outcome, they could not be easily adapted to new items, as their business logic is strongly connected to the content they process.

Then, we have the engines that drive recommendations based on user behavior. In these, a mathematical relationship is computed based on vectors that represent sessions (containing item identifiers), and the recommendations are just the application of computing methodologies between those vectors, regardless of which products or which properties they hold. Here, we talk about collaborative filtering techniques. As you might have guessed, the quality of this technique is that it does not depend on an item's content to work and so presents more scalability in comparison to content-based recommendation engines.

In reality, you'll find websites that use a combination of these two techniques, but for our recipe, we will focus on one special kind of content-filtering engine that is based on the number of times an item is visited or bought with some other item: the co-occurrence-based recommendation engine.

The intuition behind this technique is that if a user visits an item, we'll suggest that the user also have a look at all the items that other users showed interest in when they also visited that same item. For this, we'll have to maintain a data structure and co-occurrence matrix for each item that was accessed within a single browsing session.

Say, for example, that `user1` visited `item1`, `item2`, and `item3`.

The co-occurrence matrix for this example would be:

```
item1 : (item2,1), (item3,1) - that is, with item1 occurred item2
once, and item3 once
item2 : (item3,1), (item1, 1) - that is, with item2 occurred item3
once, and item1 once
item3 : (item2,1), (item1,1) - that is, whit item3 occurred item1 once
and item2 once
```

If another user, `user2`, visits `item2` and `item3`, the co-occurrence matrix would be:

```
item1 : (item2,1), (item3,1) - that is, item1 occurred with item2 only
once (in user1 session), and so it is with item3
item2 : (item3,2), (item1,1) - that is, item2 occurred twice with
item3 (in user1 and user2's sessions) but only once with item1
item3 : (item1,1),(item2,2) - that is  item3 occurred twice with
item2 (in user1 and user2's sessions), but only once with item1 (in
user1's session)
```

> Note that this is a symmetric matrix. Also, we'll be able to construct this structure live, as the events flow within sessions and we'll do just that; we are not going to process huge amount of sessions offline.

Now, how do we compute recommendations? For a user, `userR`, whom we want to suggest items to, we will take a session containing `item2`. We just have to look up the co-occurrence data structure and provide that user with suggestions based on the knowledge about any items that have been visited along with `item2` during any other browsing session. The user visited `item2`, so we suggest the user to visit `item3` (with a score of 2) and `item1` (with a score of 1). Note how the number of co-occurrences can be useful in sorting the recommendations; actually, the more often items are visited together, the more likely they may be tied.

Now, what if a session has multiple items? Say, for example, a new user, `user3`, introduced a new item to the matrix and visited `item3` and `item5`. Our co-occurrence structure now would be:

```
item1 : (item2,1), (item3,1) - that is, item1 occurred with item2 only
once (in user1 session), and so it is with item3
item2 : (item3,2), (item1,1) - that is, item2 occurred twice with
item3(in user1 and user2's sessions) but only once with item1
item3 : (item1,1),(item2,2),(item5,1) - that is  item3 occurred twice
with item2(in user1 and user2's sessions), but only once with item1
(in user1's session) and only once with item3 (as per user3 session)
item5:(item3,1) - That is item5 occurred only once with item3 (in
user3's session)
```

The user `userR` now visited `item5`. His session so far contains `item2` and `item5`. What should we recommend to him next? We first compute recommendations for `item2`, which are `(item3,2)` and `(item1,1)`, and then we compute a recommendation for `item5`, which is `(item3,1)`. Now, we just sum up this vector:

```
(item3,2) , (item1,1) + (item3,1)
=
(item3,3),(item1,1)
```

This is what we'd recommend `userR`.

Note that as far as recommendation computation is concerned, we do not have to carry on heavy offline matrix operations; we just have to access a few rows referenced by item identifiers (which will be efficiently handled by Clojure maps, in which you can access values in constant time). In this way, our recommendation engine will be designed and we can make it live so that it reacts as the events flow in.

Lastly, our users can have preferences for the items they access, that is, they can visit a particular item multiple times, and they can rate products as well. Anyway, our session may contain items with preferences, as follows:

```
5 item2 + 3 item1
```

Now, you may ask, how should we handle preferences expressed in this manner? Well, first of all, preferences as such have no impact on the computation of the co-occurrence matrix (unless the preference has been yielded by multiple accesses on an item, in which case, the matrix would have been updated, as we would have had processed these corresponding events anyway). However, a preference does have effect on the recommendation computation. Now, you'd have to sum up the co-occurrence vectors and multiply them by the corresponding item preference. Let's take an example, and assume that `userR` has:

```
5item2, 3item1
```

Now, the recommendation would be computed, as follows:

```
    5 X (item3,2) , (item1,1)  + 3 X (item3,1)
=
    (item3,10),(item1,5)
    (item3,3)
=   (item3,13),(item1,5)
```

Note, finally, that co-occurrence is just one possible measure, among many others, of how to interpret the relationship between two elements. In order to have a parameterized recommender, we will use a generic notion of a similarity map, in which we add 1 to the relationship to two elements, whenever they occur together. You could, for example, use a similarity map containing a measure of content similarity between two items, so that the following implementation can be used
for a content-based recommendation.

How to do it...

1. First of all, we are going to import `clojure.set`, as we will use a set of operations in our implementation:

```clojure
(ns recipe13.core
  (:require [clojure.set]))
```

2. Now, we will build the `corr-matrix-delta` function, which takes an item and a similarity map and computes the difference to be applied to a correlation map. This difference is a line that contains these items that refer to the other items they are related to, and some other lines, one for each of those items that refer to the first item that we were talking about. This "delta" will be applied to the correlation matrix as items are visited, so the former is incrementally kept up to date. Note that we are talking about correlation maps and not co-occurrence specifically, as we parameterize by `sim-map`, which tells us how to interpret the occurrence of two items together:

```clojure
(defn corr-matrix-delta
  [this-item
   sim-map]
  (let [s-sim-map (dissoc sim-map this-item)]
;; in case sim contains the item, we remove it
    (if (seq s-sim-map)
;; if this map contains elements
      (let [line-this-item {this-item s-sim-map}
;; we generate the line this-item : item1 similarity1
;; item2 similarity2...
            lines-sim-map (into {} (map (fn [[k v]]
                                          {k {this-item v}})
```

```
                                    s-sim-map))]
;; and the lines item1 : this-item similarity1
;; item2 : this-item similarity2
  (conj lines-sim-map line-this-item))
;; end we return that delta to be applied when we receive
;; this item and we had that similarity map
{})))
```

3. Now, we apply the delta that we just constructed to a correlation matrix, so that we end up with an updated correlation information each and every time we receive a new item:

```
(defn update-corr-matrix
  [corr-matrix
   this-item
   sim-map]
  (merge-with (partial merge-with +)
                ;; we apply delta, adding to the items
                ;; we already have the new values that
                ;; came along with this new item occurrence
                corr-matrix
                (corr-matrix-delta this-item sim-map)))
```

4. Now, we will devise a function to compute the co-occurrence matrix. Given a session, we compute a similarity matrix that assigns exactly 1 to each item in a browsing session; that is to say that we may add 1 to the number of times this item occurred with each and every item of a given session:

```
(defn update-cooc-matrix
  [corr-matrix
   this-item
   session-map]
  (let [cooc-sim (zipmap (keys session-map)
                          (repeat 1))]
    ;; cooc-sim is a particular similarity map:
    ;; we add 1 to the relation this-item->a session item
    ;; so to compute the times they occurred together
    (update-corr-matrix corr-matrix this-item cooc-sim)))
```

5. Given an item and a preference, we give a recommendation for this item based on the related entries in the correlation matrix (which is a co-occurrence matrix constructed as explained in the previous step, assigning an exact amount of 1 as similarity between a particular item and every product that has been visited during some particular session). To clarify the implementation, we use a utility function to apply a function to map the values:

```
(defn apply-fn-to-map-vals
"applies function f to map m values and returns the resulting map"
  [f m]
  (into  {}
         (map (fn [[k v]] [k (f v)]) m)))


(defn recommend-for-an-item
  [corr-matrix
   this-item
   pref]
  (if-let [items->this-item (corr-matrix this-item) ]
;; if we find an entry in this correlation matrix for this item
;; We begin by getting the elements related to this element
;; in the correlation matrix
    (->> items->this-item
         (apply-fn-to-map-vals (partial * pref)))
;; we multiply the correlation by the preference
;; else we return an empty map
    {}))
```

6. Finally, we build the recommendation for a complete preferences map, or a particular user session with preferences:

```
(defn recommend-for-a-prefs-map
  [corr-matrix
   pref-maps]
  (->> pref-maps
       (map  (fn [[item pref]] (recommend-for-an-item corr-matrix
                                                      item
                                                      pref)))
;; We compute a recommendation for every item taking
;; in consideration it preference
       (reduce (partial merge-with +))))
;; And then we merge them into a single map to come up with the
;; final recommendation
```

7. Let's now see our recommender in action. Assume that we have two users; the first one clicks on `item1` and then on `item2`. The second one begins by visiting `item3` and then `item4`. As our system interprets events as they flow by, it is important to replay the sessions as they are constructed:

```
(def cooc-matrix   (-> {}
                                  (update-cooc-matrix :item1 {})
                         (update-cooc-matrix :item2 {:item1 2})
                                  (update-cooc-matrix :item3 {})
                         (update-cooc-matrix :item4 {:item3 2}))))
```

8. Now, let's assume that another user accessed `item1` and `item3` with preferences as per the preferences map shown in the next example. What would the system recommend for this user? The system would recommend the recommendation computed by the addition of the two recommendations yielded by the first and second sessions:

```
(def user3-prefs-map {:item1 2 :item3 4})
(recommend-for-a-prefs-map cooc-matrix user3-prefs-map)
;; => {:item4 4, :item2 2}
```

Resolving cost and profit optimization problems

For this recipe, we will study optimization problems. For these, you are given a set of constraints on some variables, say:

```
4x+3y < 30
2x+4y < 10
```

You are then asked to maximize or minimize a function of these variables, (if constraints are inferior, then you'll have to maximize and vice versa), for example:

```
max(z=13 x + 7 y)
```

This is called the objective function. Generally speaking, such problems are called **linear programs**, and the algorithm used for resolving these is called the simplex algorithm.

However, the simplex algorithm operates on real variables, that is, the variables that take real values. This is problematic if the solution to the problem can only be a compound of natural numbers. For instance, let's assume that some bakery calls you to help them optimize their profit. They tell you that they produce three kinds of products: bread, croissants, and muffins. The bread takes 2 units of sugar and 4 units of flour, the croissant takes 1 unit of sugar and 1 unit of flour, whereas the muffin needs 3 units of sugar and 3 units of flour each. Every day, the bakery has 40 units of sugar and 50 units of flour to make its products. They finally let you know that they sell the bread for 1 dollar each, the croissant for 2 dollars, and the muffin for 3 dollars each. To help them maximize their income, you begin by putting on paper the linear program relative to their data:

2 Nbread + 1 Ncroissants + 3 Nmuffins <= 40 (The sugar cost constraint)

4 Nbread + 1 Ncroissants + 3 Nmuffins <= 50 (The flour cost constraint)

Max(Z=1 Nbread + 2 Ncroissants + 3 Nmuffins) (The objective function)

If you use the simplex algorithm to resolve this problem, you'd probably come up with real number solutions, which would clearly not be relevant in our case. Telling the bakery to produce 5,666 loaves of bread a day to optimize their profits makes very little sense. Besides, rounding up the real values determined by the simplex algorithm will not help you attain the optimal solution.

So, you clearly need a different approach to resolve these discrete programs that can only have solutions with natural number components. As you are seeking integer results, you may be tempted to try, one by one, all possible integer values for every possible variable (bread, croissants, and muffins) to see where your objective might be optimal. Doing so, you'd be practically combining infinite possibilities for three variables, and this would not be an approach that would lead us to a result in a reasonable amount of time.

The branch and bound algorithm comes in handy in such situations. In branch and bound, we consider that the enumeration of all the results follows a tree structure, as shown in the following figure:

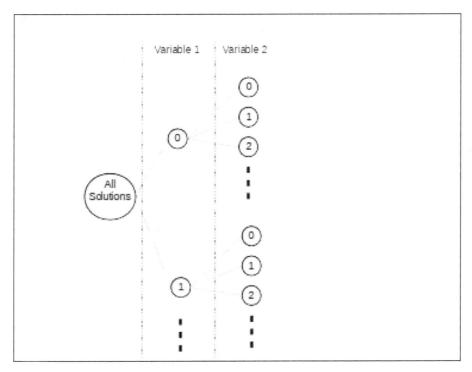

The solution tree structure in branch and bound

The root of the tree is labeled as **All solutions**, and as you enumerate the possible values for each of the variables, you go through several internal nodes. When you reach an internal node, we say that you have reached a partial solution, that is, you have not yet enumerated values for all your variables. When you reach a leaf, you have an actual enumerated possible solution, as at that point, you have assigned a value to every variable. So, enumerating all possible solutions is a matter of developing a tree like this one, and this operation is called **branching**.

The main point in branch and bound is to avoid exploring all solution trees. This algorithm does so by providing a mechanism that makes it possible for us to decide, at each node of the tree, whether going deeper by branching from that node is worth the hassle. So, we try to come up with a heuristic, which is optimistic enough, so its value, by all means, is better than the actual value of the objective function—if you decide to go deeper until you reach an actual solution. We call this the bounding function. At every stage of exploration, we compare the value of the bounding function with the best value of any objective function of a complete solution that we were able to reach; if it is no better, and knowing that it is optimistic (so, it surely is better than the reality), we abandon this branch and try another value for the variable. So, now you understand why the name of the method for the operation you'd perform when exploring the tree is branch, and why the name of the method when you compute the bounding function, and decide to cut off a whole branch of a tree knowing that it cannot help improve your objective, is bound.

It is important to note that we also abandon any solution that is not feasible - for instance, if at a particular stage we observe that a partial solution violates one constraint, then there's no point in further exploring that branch. Hence, you need to explore the next branch.

A very important aspect of this algorithm is the choice of your bounding function. This is domain-specific, and you must choose a function with creativity in order to be sure that you efficiently attain a solution; that is, you need to cut off as many non-useful branches as possible.

Now, we call the latest, best-known solution: the incumbent. This is a feasible solution, which we were able to attain (all bounding functions along the way were better than the previous incumbent).

We'll stop our algorithm when we detect that no solution will ever provide for a better bounding function value than we already have -that is, we know that every non explored path down the solutions tree is neither feasible nor shows a worst bounding function result.

Now, back to our bakery problem - which would be a good bounding function? We chose the one that operates as described in the following section:

Given a particular position in the solutions' tree, compute the remaining amount of flour and sugar, and with this amount of materials, bake as many pastries as you can regardless of the constraint that you didn't explore in the tree. As you have many constraints, take the maximum values determined for each pastry at every constraint level. Compute the resulting objective function; this will be your bounding value. Let me explain this by an example.

Suppose that you are at the node `Nbread=10`. Now, your discrete program reads:

```
20 + 1 Ncroissants + 3 Nmuffins <= 40 (The sugar cost constraint)
40 + 1 Ncroissants + 3 Nmuffins <= 50 (The flour cost constraint)
The sugar that remains : 40 - 20 = 20
The flour that remains : 50 - 40 = 10
possible Ncroissants : 20 / 1 =20 or 10 /1 = 10 => Ncroissants = 20
possible Nmuffins : 20 / 3 ~ 6 or 10 / 1 ~ 3 => Nmuffins = 6
bounding function value at node Nbreads = 10 =>  1 * 10 + 2 * 20 + 3 *
6 = 68
```

So, the bounding function of the node `Nbreads=10` is `68`. You'd only continue to explore this branch if it's better than the incumbent.

For our implementation, a branch in the tree is a vector of the values that we've explored so far. Besides, we consider that if a node is not feasible, then we come back to the previous node, as there is no way that adding values to it would make it feasible. For instance, if the vector `[3,2, 1]` is not feasible, adding `0` to it, as in `[3,2,1,0]`, does not make sense; there's no point continuing in this branch as : `[3,2,2]`, `[3,2,3...]` would not lower the value; so, we jump back to the node `[3,3]`.

We consider that our exploration is done when we reach the root; if we are at `[]`, we consider that we've reached a solution that is not feasible no matter which node you explore.

How to do it...

1. We will begin with some functions for branching and go up in the tree:

```
(defn new-branch
  [p-solution]
  ;; a new branch explores a
  ;; new branch, that is a new
  ;; value for the next variable
  (conj p-solution 0))

(defn next-solution-in-branch
  [p-solution]
  ;; next solution in branch is
  ;; the next value in the same level,
  ;; not adding any new levels
  (conj (pop p-solution)
        (inc (peek p-solution))))

(defn back-in-tree
  [p-solution]
  ;; back in tree gets to
```

```
;; the upper level node
;; which is done by
;; getting the node vector
;; minus its head
(pop p-solution))
```

2. Our problem definition is:

```
;; constraints => [{:coefs [1 3 2 4] :constraint < :limit 10} ...]
;; The objective  =>    [2 3 1 2]
```

3. Now we are going to define some functions to qualify the solutions that we came across during our branching phases, as well as defining a function that computes the objective value of a particular solution:

```
(defn is-conform-constraint?
  [constraint-direction solution a-constraint]
  ;; Tests if a single constraint is verified
  (let [{:keys [coefs limit]} a-constraint
        solution-val (reduce +
                             (map * coefs solution))]
    (constraint-direction solution-val limit)))


(defn is-realisable-solution?
  ;; Tests if the solution is realisable,
  ;; that is, every constraint is conform
  [solution constraints constraint-direction]
  (->> constraints
       (map (partial is-conform-constraint?
                     constraint-direction
                     solution
                     ))
       (every? true?)))


(defn valid-constraint-coefs?
  ;; in our problem domain, our coefficients
  ;; must be positive
  [a-constraint]
  (let [{:keys [coefs limit]} a-constraint]
    (and  (every? (partial < 0) coefs)
          (>  limit 0))))


(defn valid-objective?
  ;; and all the coefficients in the
  ;; objective function as well
  [objective]
```

```
(every? (partial < 0) objective ))

(defn objective-val
  ;; Computes the objective value for a
  ;; particular solution
  [solution objective]
  (reduce +
          (map *
               solution
               objective)))
```

4. With all these functions at hand, let's define branch-n-bound. We will need a utility function, complete-p-solution-w-zeroes, so that we can test whether a node is a realizable solution before diving deeper:

```
(defn complete-p-solution-w-zeroes
  [p-solution nvars]
  ;; given a partial solution, and
  ;; the total number of variables nvars
  ;; yields a vector with partial solution
  ;; and remaining vars at 0; this will be used
  ;; to test if the current branch is realisable.
  ;; If not, we go up in the tree, no point in
  ;; branching in this direction.
  (into p-solution (repeat (- nvars (count p-solution))
                           0)))

(defn branch-n-bound
  [constraints
   constraint-direction
   n-vars
   objective
   bounding-fn
   incumbent-default]
  {:pre [(every? valid-constraint-coefs? constraints)
         (valid-objective? objective)]}
  ;; We verify that our problem description is
  ;; consistent
  (loop [solution (new-branch  [])
         incumbent []]
    (let [sol-size (count solution)
      sol-w-zeroes (complete-p-solution-w-zeroes solution n-vars)
          incumbent-val (if (empty? incumbent )
                          incumbent-default
  ;; We have not found an incumbent yet,
```

```
;; set it at a default value
                            (objective-val incumbent objective))]
;; or compute its value
      (if  (< sol-size n-vars )
;; this is a partial solution
        (if  (not  (is-realisable-solution? sol-w-zeroes
                                            constraints
                                            constraint-direction))
;; This branch is not realisable, we move up in the tree,

          (let [s-parent (back-in-tree solution)]
            (if (not (empty? s-parent))
;; if it is not empty, we branch from the upper node
              (recur (next-solution-in-branch s-parent) incumbent)
                        ;; if it is empty, we're done,
                        ;; we return the current incumbent
              incumbent))
        ;; This solution is realisable, we can explore further.
        ;; Let's see if the bound function does better
        ;; than our incumbent,
        (let [solution-bound-val (bounding-fn constraints
                                              n-vars
                                              solution
                                              objective)]
          (if (or (and (not (empty? incumbent))
                        ((complement constraint-direction)
solution-bound-val
                            incumbent-val))
                  (empty? incumbent))
            (recur (new-branch solution) incumbent)
              ;; we are better than the incumbent,
              ;; we continue exploring in this branch
            (recur (next-solution-in-branch solution)
incumbent))))
        ;; we are not better than the incumbent,
        ;; we try another node in the same level

    ;; Here we reached a complete solution. If it is realizable,
    ;; and if it is better than incumbent,
    ;; we take it as the new incumbent,
    ;; and recur with the next solution in this branch
        (if (is-realisable-solution? solution constraints
constraint-direction)
            (if (or    ((complement constraint-direction)
```

```
                    (objective-val solution objective)
                        incumbent-val)
                    (empty? incumbent))
            (recur (next-solution-in-branch solution)
                    solution)
        ;; We have a new incumbent
          (recur (next-solution-in-branch solution)
                  incumbent))
        ;; this solution isn't better than the new incumbent,
        ;; we try the next node under the same branch

        ;; It is not realisable, so we try the next
        ;; node starting from the parent node
        (let [s-parent (back-in-tree solution)]
          (recur (next-solution-in-branch s-parent)
                  incumbent)))))))
```

5. Finally, let's define the bounding function for our bakery problem:

```
(defn baker-rem-vars
  [a-constraint
   n-vars
   p-solution]
  ;; this function computes the
  ;; values for non explored vars
  ;; in a partial solution, and determines
  ;; their optimistic possible values
  ;; for a given constraint
  (let [{:keys [coefs limit]} a-constraint
        n-fixed-vars (count p-solution)
        consumed-by-fixed-vars (reduce +
                                        (map *
                                            p-solution
                                            coefs))
        remaining (- limit consumed-by-fixed-vars)
        free-vars (subvec coefs n-fixed-vars)
        free-vars-optimistic-assign (mapv (comp int (partial /
  remaining ))
                                            free-vars )]
     (into p-solution free-vars-optimistic-assign)))

 (defn baker-bounding-fn
  [constraints
   n-vars
   p-solution
```

```
      objective]
;; Given a set of constraints,
;; an objective and a partial solution
;; This function computes the bounding function value
;; for our bakery problem : the max of the possible values
;; that every variable can take from the remaining
;; resource at every constraint's level
(let [completions (mapv  #(baker-rem-vars %
                                          n-vars p-solution)
                         constraints)
      var-values-in-cols (map (fn  [col] (for [line completions]
                                           (get line col)))
                              (range n-vars))
      optimistic-solution (mapv (partial apply max)
                                var-values-in-cols)]
  (objective-val optimistic-solution objective)))
```

6. Now, let's help our friend the baker and resolve his optimization problem. We will
    begin by defining the constraints:

    ```
    (def baker-constraints [{:coefs [2 1 3] :constraint <= :limit 40}
                            {:coefs [4 1 3] :constraint
    <= :limit 50}])
    ```

7. Now, we define the objective function:

    ```
    (def baker-objective [1 2 3])
    ```

8. The best schedule for this bakery is as follows; now we know that the baker is better
    off making nothing but croissants!

    ```
    (branch-n-bound baker-constraints
    <= 3 baker-objective baker-bounding-fn 0)
    ;; => [0 40 0]
    ```

Finding optimal paths in a graph

Consider that you are driving back home. You have in mind information about roads that
you need to take in order to go from your office to your sweet home, and you can provide a
measure of time you'll spend on each one of these roads, considering the distance covered
and the amount of traffic you'll likely run into by taking it. How are you going to determine the
best path home? This problem of yours falls under the class of problems to find the shortest
path, and for this recipe, we are going to solve this problem using the **Dijkstra algorithm**.

Given a graph, the Dijkstra's algorithm proceeds by visiting one currently unvisited node at every iteration, considering all its neighbors, and computing values that represent distances to these neighbors if one used the current node to reach them. If, for any neighbor, the value computed is better than any value already held by it, that is, the value is already computed when it was previously visited by another neighboring node, then the value of this particular neighbor is updated by the better value and its parent node is set to this current node.

At the end, when we reach the target node, we stop the algorithm. From that target, we go all way back and access the parent nodes until we reach the starting node. The path built this way is the best (shortest) path from the start to the target.

The beauty of this algorithm lies in its simplicity; actually, the Dijkstra algorithm designed it in as little as 20 minutes with practically no effort, but it is important to say that he actually rediscovered it some time after Prim, who himself devised it 29 years after Jarnik.

How to do it...

1. First, let's describe the two data structures that we are going to use in the Dijkstra algorithm. We have the graph data structure that holds information about the nodes that represent the city intersections for the roads you might take:

   ```
   ;; graph -> {:s {:a 2 :b 3} a {:b 1 :c 3} :c {:t 20 :d 4} }
   ```

2. We also have the path data structure, which will hold the result of the Dijkstra algorithm:

   ```
   ;; paths -> {:a {:dist 4 :prev :v}} ...
   ```

3. Now, we need a function that takes a node, a particular neighbor, the distance of the node from a source, the distance of the neighbor from that node, and the current distance in a path ; checks if the distance to the neighbor using that particular node is any better than what was stored in the current distance in path, and returns it if it is the case.

   ```
   (defn update-dist-of-neighbor
     [node
      neighbor
      dist-from-source
      dist-from-node
      current-dist-in-path]
     (let [dist-through-node (+ dist-from-source dist-from-node)]
       (if (or   (nil? current-dist-in-path)
                 (and   (not (nil? current-dist-in-path))
                        (< dist-through-node current-dist-in-path)))
         {neighbor {:dist dist-through-node :prev node}})))
   ```

4. Now, we can build a function that processes all the neighbors of a given node based on the graph information and the distances computed so far that are held in the path:

```
(defn process-node
  [graph
   current-node
   path]
  (let [neighbors (get graph current-node)
        dist-from-source (if-let [curnode-in-path (get path
current-node)]
                              (get curnode-in-path :dist)
                              0)
        ;; This is the source node, so we'll give it 0 as distance
        new-path (->> neighbors ;; for each of its neighbors
                      (map (fn [[neighbor dist-to-cur-node]]
                             (update-dist-of-neighbor current-node
                                                       neighbor
                                                       dist-from-source
                                                       dist-to-cur-node
                                                       (get (get
path neighbor) :dist))))
                      ;; we'll compute the new distance and previous node
                      ;; using the utility function (update-dist-of-neighbor)
                      (into path))]
        ;; which we'll return as new-path
    new-path))
```

5. Now we can run the Dijkstra's algorithm, which will visit all the graph's nodes using the function we just devised:

```
(defn dijkstra
  [graph]
  (loop [remaining-vertices (keys graph)
         path {}]
    (if (seq remaining-vertices)
      (let [current-vertex (first remaining-vertices)]
        ;; for every node we process its neighbors
        ;; using process-node
        (recur (rest remaining-vertices)
               (process-node graph current-vertex path)))
      path)))
```

6. Finally, we must process the resulting path to return the shortest path from a starting point to a target. The following function, after calling the Dijkstra's algorithm on a graph, walks the resultant data structure path all the way back using the :prev references and returns the shortest path between two nodes:

```
(defn shortest-path
  [graph source target]
  (let [dijkstra-shortest-paths (dijkstra graph)]
    ;; we compute the shortest paths
    (loop [new-target (get dijkstra-shortest-paths target)
    ;; We begin from target
           path [target]]
      (let [next-new-target (get new-target :prev)]
    ;; and get back to the previous node
        (cond (nil? next-new-target) :error
    ;; we did not find a :prev reference
              (= next-new-target source) (into [source] path)
    ;; we are done,
    ;; we return the path
              :default (recur (get dijkstra-shortest-paths
                                   next-new-target)
    ;; we recur using the previous node
    ;; and adding it to the result path
                              (into [next-new-target] path)))))))
```

7. Time to help you get back home as quickly as possible. Let's assume your city intersection's graph looks like:

```
(def city-ints-graph {:s {:a 1 :b 2} :a {:c 3 :d 1 } :b {:t 20} :c
{:t 3} :d {:t 15}})
```

8. Your best path home going from :s to :t is:

```
(shortest-path city-ints-graph :s :t)
;; => [:s :a :c :t]
```

Summarizing texts by extracting the most representative sentences

In this recipe, we are going to use an extractive method to build a summary out of a set of text documents. By extractive, we mean that rather than drawing any knowledge from the source documents in order to rephrase it in a more concise way, we'll try to detect the most salient sentences in those documents and show these as the summary of the text.

The algorithm we are going to use is somewhat inspired by Google's PageRank and is labeled as LexRank. The spirit behind it is if we try to represent every document sentence as a vector, we shall come up with a graph that represents all of these sentences tied together. Every edge drawn between each couple of sentences is weighted by the distance between these two sentences. If any two distances are close enough, we can say that they are connected. Then, the logic we find in PageRank applies. We define the degree of each sentence as the number of the others that are connected to it, and the most representative sentences are those who have the highest degrees.

Now, how do you represent a sentence as a vector? We use a common measure in order to represent text as vectors: **term frequency inverse document frequency (TF-IDF)**.

Term frequency (TF) is the measure of how many times a particular word occurs in a sentence. In order to get rid of the bias caused by words that are frequently used in language, such as "the", "a", "is...", we multiply the TF of a word by its **inverse document frequency (IDF)**, that is, a measure of how often a particular word is present across all the documents at our disposal. This way, the most characteristic words gain more weight in the vector that represents a sentence. Mathematically, TFIDF is computed using the following formula:

TFIDF = TF * IDF

Here, *TF* refers to the term frequency of a word in a sentence and IDF

IDF refers to log (the number of documents/number of documents where this term occurs).

Now, how do you compute the distance between two sentences represented by TFIDF vectors? In general, a good measure of the distance between two text documents is the cosine similarity, which gives us an idea about the angle between the two vectors; indeed, two sentences may have different TFIDF coordinates, but will more or less point in the same direction, which can be interpreted as having their different word ratios pretty close together. The cosine similarity between two sentences represented by their TFIDF vectors is computed as shown in the following formula:

$$\frac{\sum_{w \in x,y} \mathrm{tf}_{w,x} \mathrm{tf}_{w,y} (\mathrm{idf}_w)^2}{\sqrt{\sum_{x_i \in x} (\mathrm{tf}_{x_i,x} \mathrm{idf}_{x_i})^2} \times \sqrt{\sum_{y_i \in y} (\mathrm{tf}_{y_i,y} \mathrm{idf}_{y_i})^2}}$$

In the cosine similarity formula, *x* and *y* are two sentences, and *xi* and *yi*, respectively, contain the word in *x* and *y*.

The method that consists of the computation of the degrees of sentences, where the most salient sentences are those with the higher degrees, is called centrality-based sentence salience. If you build a matrix that has all the document's sentences in both columns and rows, you write only the cosine similarity to be higher than a given threshold, and you give zero elsewhere; then, you'd have to count the number of each non-zero element at each one of your matrix row (or column) and you'd end up with the measure of the degree of each sentence of our documents. This is called degree centrality of each sentence.

However, degree centrality alone may not yield good quality summaries. If you consider all the sentences that contributed to some degree computation as being equally important, you might get a biased result in certain situations. Consider, for example, a set of documents that are all related, but only one of them is different and is about another topic. You wouldn't want a sentence from this "black sheep" document to end up in your final summary. However, if any of this particular document's sentences get a high degree from other sentences contained in that same document, it will, erroneously, be part of your summary.

One way to avoid this situation is to include, along with the number of sentences, some assessment of the "quality" of these sentences, in the process of computing centrality degree: If we consider the close sentences that yield the centrality degree as a voter, we will also have to take into account the centrality degree of that very voter as a measure of how relevant to the vote it may be. The idea can be simply rephrased to consider that every node has a centrality and that we are going to distribute its centrality to all its neighbors. This can be expressed by:

Centrality (node) =The Sum, for every adjacent-node to node Centrality (adjacent-node) / degree (adjacent-node)

The preceding formula is mathematically equivalent to resolving the matricial equation.

p(This is exponential)B=p(This is exponential), where *p* is the centrality we are seeking for and *B* is the adjacency matrix we determined by considering the similarity between each couple of sentences, whose elements are divided by each corresponding row's sum.

Using some mathematical background and taking inspiration from the dampening factor usage in Google's PageRank method, which is beyond the scope of this book, we will resolve the preceding equation by an iterative method called the power-method (here, *M* is a special matrix [stochastic, irreducible, and aperiodic] - and adjacency matrix B has these properties - and *N* is the size of this matrix):

```
p0 = vector of  (1/N ,...,1/N)  (N times)
t=0
repeat
  t=t+1
 pt   = Mtpt - 1
 error = ||pt - pt-1 ||
until error is inferior to a given threshold
return pt
```

Pt will be then our quality centrality vector and it will give for each sentence a measure of how salient it is. To build a summary, we then only have to take some sentences with the highest corresponding values in *Pt*.

> For a more thorough explanation of the theoretical background behind LexRank, refer to the original publication, which you can find at
>
> `http://www.cs.cmu.edu/afs/cs/project/jair/pub/volume22/erkan04a-html/erkan04a.html`.

How to do it...

1. For starters, let's import some facilities that we'll make use of in this recipe:

```
(ns recipe16.core
    (:import (java.io BufferedReader FileReader))
    (:import java.io.File)
    ;; So we are able to read our text documents
    (:refer-clojure :exclude [* - + == /])
    (:require [clojure.java.io :refer (file)]
             [clojure.string :refer (split)]
    ;; so we are able to use matrices operations
             [clojure.core.matrix :refer :all]
             [clojure.core.matrix.operators :refer :all]))
```

2. Now, we are going to count the words in the documents in order to compute IDF. Here, documents must be sets of words:

```
(defn word-in-nb-documents
    [word documents]
    (->> documents
        (filter #(contains?  % word))
        count))

(defn idf-words
    [documents]
    (let [N (count documents)
          all-docs-words (apply clojure.set/union
                                (mapv set documents))]
      (->> all-docs-words
          (map (fn[w]  {w (Math/log (/ N
                                    (word-in-nb-documents w
documents)))}))
          (into {})))))
```

3. Now, let's extract the sentences in documents that are contained in a given directory:

```clojure
(defn sentences-in-document
  "This function extracts the sentences in a particular document"
  [file]
  (with-open [rdr (BufferedReader. (FileReader.  file))]
    (->> (line-seq rdr)
         (map clojure.string/trim)
         (mapcat #(split % #"[.|!|?|:]+"))
         (mapv clojure.string/lower-case))))


(defn gen-docs-w-sentences
  "This function takes a path and generates a vector of
  a vector of sentences, as per the documents containing
  them"
  [path]
  (let [files (.listFiles (File. path))]
    (mapv sentences-in-document
          files)))
```

4. At this particular point, we can consider computing TFIDF of the sentences that we just extracted:

```clojure
(defn words-in-document-sentences
  "This function extracts the words from all document sentences "
  [document-sentences]
  (mapcat #(split % #"[\s|,|;]") document-sentences ))


(defn gen-idf-map-from-docs-sentences
  "This function generates a map with all words IDF"
  [documents-w-sentences]
  (let [documents-w-words
(map set (map words-in-document-sentences
                                       documents-w-sentences))]
    (idf-words documents-w-words)))


;; a sentence is a vector of words.
(defn tfidf-vector-from-sentence
;; for this one you must compute idf beforehand
  [idf-map sentence]
  (let [sentence-words (split sentence #"[\s|,|;|:]+")
        tf-sentence    (->> sentence-words
                            (map (fn [k] {k 1}))
                            (reduce (partial merge-with +)))]
    ;; We compute  the TF for the words based on their
    ;; frequency in every sentence
```

```
(->> tf-sentence
     (map (fn [[k v]] { k (* v (get idf-map k))} ))
     ;; and then we generate TFIDF maps for each
     ;; sentence, referred by words. These
     ;; will be the vectors representing our sentences
     (into {})))))
```

5. Now, we must compute the cosine-similarity:

```
(defn cosine-similarity
  [tfidf-sentence1 tfidf-sentence2]
  (let [common-words (clojure.set/intersection
(set (keys tfidf-sentence1))
                                   (set (keys tfidf-sentence2)))
        ;; we use common words because we don't have to multiply
        ;; by 0
        s1-common (select-keys tfidf-sentence1 common-words)
        s2-common (select-keys tfidf-sentence2 common-words)

        Ss1Xs2 (reduce + (vals  (merge-with * s1-common s2-common)))
        sqrt-Ss1pow2 (->> (vals tfidf-sentence1)
                          (map  #(Math/pow % 2))
                          (reduce +  )
                          Math/sqrt)

        sqrt-Ss2pow2 (->> (vals tfidf-sentence2)
                          (map  #(Math/pow % 2))
                          (reduce +  )
                          Math/sqrt)]
    (if (every? (comp not zero?)
                [sqrt-Ss1pow2 sqrt-Ss2pow2] )
      (/ Ss1Xs2 (* sqrt-Ss1pow2 sqrt-Ss2pow2))
      0)))
```

6. We will also design the power method computing function:

```
(defn power-method
  [mat error]
  (let [size (dimension-count mat 0)]
    (loop [p (matrix (into [] (repeat size
                                        (/ 1 size))))]
      (let [new-p (mmul (transpose mat) p)
            sigma (distance new-p p)]
        (if (< sigma error)
          new-p
          (recur new-p))))))
```

7. Now, we can put together the LexRank function:

```
(defn lexrank
  [path
   cosine-threshold
   lexrank-error
   topN]
  (let [sentences-by-docs (gen-docs-w-sentences path)
        idf-map (gen-idf-map-from-docs-sentences
                  sentences-by-docs)
     all-sentences (into [] (mapcat identity sentences-by-docs))
        sentences-w-tfidf (into [] (reduce concat
                                    (for [s sentences-by-docs]
                              (map (partial tfidf-vector-from-sentence
                                                idf-map)
                                        s))))
     ;; We begin by representing all of our sentences as TFIDF vectors
        cent-raw-matrix (matrix (into [] (for [i sentences-w-tfidf]
                                 (into [] (for [j sentences-w-tfidf]
                               (let [cos-sim-i-j(cosine-similarity i j)]
                                  (if (>= cos-sim-i-jcosine-threshold)
                                                 cos-sim-i-j
                                                 0)))))))
           ;; We build a centrality raw matrix as the relationship
           ;; between every couple of sentences.
           ;; if similarity is superior than threshold,
           ;; we put it for the corresponding sentences,
           ;; else, we put zero.
           degrees (->> (rows cent-raw-matrix)
                        (mapv (partial reduce +)))
     ;; We compute the degrees for every row,
     ;; as the number of not null elements
           centrality-matrix (matrix (into []
                                      (for [i (range (count
degrees))]
                                      (/ (get-row cent-raw-matrix i)
                                                 (get degrees i)))))
        ;; We compute the matrix labeled B in the description,
        ;; dividing each element by the degree of the row
        lexrank-vector (power-method centrality-matrix lexrank-error)
        ;; We apply the powermethod
        lexrank-v-w-indices (zipmap (iterate inc 0) lexrank-vector)]
        ;; We assign indices to the sentences in the lexrank vector
        ;; so we are able to retrieve them
        (->> (sort-by val > lexrank-v-w-indices)
```

```
        (take topN)
        (map #(get % 0))
;; and we show the sentences corresponding to
;; the topN first highest LexRank Scores
        (map #(get all-sentences %)))))
```

8. Now, we need some text to sum this up. Create a folder named `test-documents` under your project folder and put these short extracts in these files:

   ❑ `test1.txt`: In this blog post, we will walk you through the different steps that are necessary to get you started with Docker Compose and show you how to use it.

   ❑ `tets2.txt`: To demonstrate the benefits of Docker Compose, we will create a simple Node.js "Hello World" application, which will run on 3 Docker Node. js containers. HTTP requests will be distributed to these Node.js nodes by an `HAProxy` instance running on another Docker container.

   ❑ `test3.txt`: Compose is a tool used to define and run complex applications with Docker. With compose, you can define a multicontainer application in a single file and then spin your application up in a single command, which does everything that needs to be done to get it running.

   ❑ Run the following function call in your REPL to get the three most-representative sentences of your documents:

   ```
   (lexrank "test-documents" 0.2 0.1 3)
   ```

   In this blog post, we will walk you through the different steps that are necessary to get you started with Docker compose and show you how to use it. "compose is a tool used to define and run complex applications with Docker >With compose, you define a multicontainer application in a single file and then spin your application up in a single command, which does everything that needs to be done to get it running.

5
Programming with Logic

In this chapter, we are going to cover a different way to derive algorithms, one that takes a highly declarative approach in order to address the problems at hand: logic programming. We'll see this paradigm in action while studying the following recipes:

- ▸ Querying a social website's data
- ▸ Designing a type inferencer
- ▸ Playing a round of checkers

Introduction

Logic programming is an interesting paradigm according to which you can express programs in terms of relations that involve some logic variables and expect results that reflect what these logical variables have to be to make sure that these relations are verified. We then speak about "goals" that "succeed", as the logical engine was able to come up some particular configuration for the logical variables so these relations are verified.

This sort of programming, also known as relational programming – as it is about relations representing goals that have to succeed - lays the foundation of an alternative way of designing algorithms. Indeed, logical (or relational) programs are highly declarative; in this, you don't tell the computer how to compute a certain result for you. Instead, you specify the rules governing the relationships between your data, and based on those, you ask for some conclusions that would have been inferred by the knowledge that you just passed on to the logical engine. Also, in logical programs, you tend to not have inputs and outputs; you just have logical variables and, according to how you arrange them in your queries, you can ask different kinds of questions by simply rearranging your input. For example, consider the following logical function:

```
(multiplio x y z)
```

This stands for a goal (or relation) which succeeds if z equals x times y.

It will succeed if you query for its result while you specify a relevant value for all 3 logical variables:

```
(multiplio 2 3 6)=>Success
```

However, if you specify that you want to know for which values of z this goal will succeed, while specifying concrete values for x and y, you are simply asking for a multiplication:

```
(multiplio 2 3 q)=> Success for q = 6
```

More interestingly, you can ask what the value of the product x might be given that y is set to 2 and that the product z is set to 6:

```
(multiplio q 3 6)=> Success for q = 2
```

So, you are able to write programs in term of relations or logic goals and specify or ask for the values of the variables that you want, knowing that the logic programming engine will try to achieve the goals and will return the combination of logical variables that allowed it to make them succeed.

Of course, when it is unable to achieve the goals, the relational kernel will give you nothing, and if it ever notices that the goals are achieved every time, it returns a value that stands for a sort of logical "everything". Look at our first example, for instance, the goal `(multiplio 2 3 6)`, which actually succeeds all the time by doing the goal multiplio, and so a program trying to process this goal would achieve (more accurately returned) success for every possible value of q.

In order to develop our relational recipes, we will use a particular miniKanren language for logic programming through its Clojure implementation, `core.logic`.

In fact, we labeled the relational function as `multiplio` (adding o to the end) as in the convention used by miniKanren authors, who named the relational functions they developed in this fashion. For more information regarding miniKanren, refer to the original dissertation by William Byrd at `http://pqdtopen.proquest.com/search.html#abstract?dispub=3380156`.

In `core.logic`, you run your queries using a special interface, as shown in the following simple example:

```
(run* [q]
   (== q 1))
```

Here, you ask `core.logic` to run a query on the logical variable q, so that the goal (`== q 1`) is verified. `==` is miniKanren's unification, that is, the mechanism that achieves a goal if the terms involved are the same. This mechanism sets q to (1) in our example. Unification is a very important operation in logical programming and is implemented up to the level of nested Clojure data structures:

```
(run* [q]
  (== [q 2] [1 2]))
```

yields (1), as we must have q at **1** so the first term of the `==` becomes [1 2] and it is unified with the second.

However, a few of you who are careful may wonder: why do we have results laid out in sequences? This is because the logical variable we are querying might happen to take multiple possible values; as a matter of fact, you can choose how many solutions you want `core.logic` to give. We did mention `run*` (star) in our query because we want all the solutions. If we only wanted to uncover the first five, we would have emitted a query as:

```
(run 5 [q]
  (== [q 2] [1 2]))
```

There is a lot that we need to underline for the use of `core.logic` and the design of logical programs, broadly speaking. We are going to cover more concepts in the first three recipes:

- ▶ **Querying a social website's data**: In this recipe, we are going to build upon a set of known facts about some social website visitors in order to draw some conclusions about how connected users behave.

- ▶ **Designing a type inferencer**: For this recipe, we will construct a system that is able to derive a program's type based on a methodology that uses unification to apply a set of inference rules: Hindley-Milner (or Damas-Milner).

- ▶ **Playing a round of checkers**: Here, we'll design a checkers solver, starting from a particular situation on a checkers board. We will strive to know what the moves an artificial brain could make to move safely on the board and to capture some of the opponent's pieces.

Querying a social website's data

Assume that you run a social networking website. On such a website, your users might be have "friendly" relations with other users. Besides, you have access to some data related to their behavior, such as information about what items they've bought from your website.

The goal of this recipe is to capture these relationships and behavior-related data, so that we are able to derive interesting facts out of them. As it turns out, it is possible in `core.logic` to specify facts that are relations between data and to query these relations in goals.

In the following section, we will answer the questions: who are a given user's friends? Who is reachable from a user's network? What did someone's friend buy? You'll even see that this last question can be turned the other way around. You'll be able to answer which users have friends that have bought a particular item, using the same previously developed routine!

How to do it...

1. For starters, here is the `ns` declaration that we must provide to be able to use the `core.logic` facilities:

```
(ns recipe17.core
  (:require [clojure.core.logic :as logic]
            [clojure.core.logic.pldb :as pldb]))
```

2. Now, we will declare two relations. A relation is a means to inform `core.logic` that we are going to use some fact's database to set a kind of schema for it. Note that we are indexing the elements of the relation, so that we are able to query it efficiently:

```
(pldb/db-rel friends ^:index a_user  ^:index another_user)
(pldb/db-rel bought ^:index a_user ^:index url)
```

3. Once these relations are declared, we can add some facts following the schemas they hold; with this, we will end up with an in-memory database of facts. We can assume that we've filled up those using some of our social website's data:

```
(def are-friends  (pldb/db
                    [friends 'rafik 'khawla]
                    [friends 'khawla 'faty]
                    [friends 'faty 'lapin]
                    [friends 'dah 'rafik]
                    [friends 'dah 'toussou]))
(def have-bought (pldb/db
                    [bought 'rafik 'pen]
                    [bought 'khawla 'computer]
                    [bought 'faty 'hello-kitty]
```

```
                            [bought 'dah 'microwave]
                            [bought 'toussou 'book]))
```

4. We can declare a piece of goal in `core.logic`. This is a function that returns some goals, which we parameterize according to our needs. For instance, the following goal function can be used to set up goals that are achieved if `user1` and `user2` are friends. As per the miniKanren tradition, we appended o to the end of that goal's function name. Note how the definition is symmetric, as we have (`friends user1 user2`), we can fairly conclude that `user1` and `user2` are mutual friends. For this, we use the `conde` operator; `conde` permits you to combine the results that are yielded upon achieving all the goals declared under its scope. conde can be seen as an OR conjunction, while laying out goals in sequences in `core.logic` is considered as a conjunction, an AND conjunction, if you will. Also note how we use the `friends` relation as goals that could be queried if we provide them inside a `core.logic` run block:

```
(defn friendo
  [user1 user2]
  (logic/conde
;; a conde is used so the two following clauses'
;; results are combined. Think of it as a sort of OR
    [(friends user1 user2)]
;; every clause in conde contains a conjunction of goals.
;; Indeed, sequences of goals
;; are always considered as conjunction, like an AND.
    [(friends user2 user1)]))
```

5. Now, we want to know what a user's friend has bought. For this, let's design `friends-boughto`. Here, we've introduced `fresh`, which is another operator of `core.logic`. It introduces new logical variables that you can use for intermediate goal resolution:

```
(defn friends-boughto
  [guy item]
;; In logic programming, we always lay out all the variables in
;; stake, not like ordinary functions, where we expect the
;; function to return a result. This is because any of these
;; logical variables can be instantiated and queried.
  (logic/fresh [f]
;; We introduce a fresh intermediate variable
    (friendo guy f)
;; To Hold the values of all friends of the guy
    (bought f item))) ;; Then we query the bought relation to see
                       ;; what items did this guy's friends buy
```

6. Let's perform some queries on the function goal that we just built. We can ask the system "what did the friends of `rafik` buy?" Here, note how the query must be rapped in the databases that we will use, `are-friends` and `have-bought`:

```
(pldb/with-db are-friends
  (pldb/with-db have-bought
    (logic/run* [q]
      (friends-boughto 'rafik q ))))

;; => (computer microwave)
```

7. Now, this is where it is going to get interesting. Remember when we talked about how the variables are resolved to achieve goals? Well this makes it possible for our program to be independent via outputs and inputs. Suppose you want to know which users have a few friends who have bought a particular item? No problem. You just specify your item and tell `core.logic` to resolve a logical variable that stands for the user whose friends have bought that item. The underlying substitution engine that resolves the goals does the rest:

```
(pldb/with-db are-friends
  (pldb/with-db have-bought
    (logic/run* [q]
      (friends-boughto q 'microwave ))))  ;; => (toussou rafik)
```

8. How about finding the entire network of friends of a particular user? We'll have to use some recursion in order to handle this case. The intuition behind the following recursive snippet is to look for the user's friends and for the friends of these friends and to combine them by using a `conde` operator. However, as it turns out, we will have to address two problems to do so. First, our goal function, as it is defined, will never stop if you ask for all the possible solutions, as it is recursively defined with a no stop condition. We can say that our program diverges. Second, some users might already be friends with some other users who are already yielded in the response, and so you might run into some redundancy, encountering these more than once. You must guarantee that the generated response is distinct. To resolve the first problem, we are going to set our goal function as `tabled`. This ensures the termination of the search (that is, avoiding divergence), as it stores in a table the different values that the variables at stake happen to take during the search, thus avoiding revisiting the same patterns over and over again. As for the second problem, we must ensure that the generated values do not contain the original user parameter that we used to launch our query:

```
(def network-of-friendo
  (logic/tabled [guy out]
      ;; as always, we lay out all the variables in stake
      ;; but this time, we use a tabled goal to avoid divergence.
          (logic/fresh [fguy]
      ;; we need a fresh variable to hold this guy's friend
              (friendo guy fguy)
      ;;  find this guy's friends
              (logic/conde
      ;; and combine the following results
              [(logic/== fguy out)]
      ;; this guy's friends
          [(network-of-friendo fguy out) (logic/!= out guy )]]))))
      ;; and those friends' friends
```

9. Now, let's pass a query for a user's network of friends:

```
(pldb/with-db are-friends
              (logic/run* [q]
                (network-of-friendo 'rafik q)))

;; => (khawla dah faty toussou lapin)
```

10. Here as well, we can interchange the variable we are querying and the input
    parameters with which we feed our query. Suppose that we want to know which
    users have a particular user in their friends' network? You can ask some of them to
    introduce you to that user. You can do this as shown in the following example:

```
(pldb/with-db are-friends
  (logic/run* [q]
    (network-of-friendo q 'rafik)))
;; => (faty lapin khawla dah toussou)
```

Designing a type inferencer

If you've ever worked with dynamically typed languages, you may have had a taste of what type inferencing is. During runtime or compile time, your program's variables and expression types are deduced to a starting set of a given rules that describe some basic type associations. Generally, this field comes along with a wide range of academic theory and its inherent mechanics can reach a high level of complexity when advanced language constructions, such as lambda expressions or polymorphic structures, come into play.

As far as our recipe is concerned, we are going to implement a subset of an algorithm known as Hindley-Milner (or Damas-Milner) to keep things simple. In Hindley-Milner, we maintain an environment of known facts about types and, at every step, some rules are used to infer new information out of that environment up until the type of our root expression is known.

Actually, we will concern ourselves with two out of the six rules that make up the Hindley-Milner algorithm: one is labeled as VAR and the other is known as APP:

▶ VAR: This is a rule that assigns to a variable the type with which it was explicitly declared. In our expressions notation, a VAR rule is depicted as the following vector:

```
[:var :x :int]
```

This shall be translated to:

```
[:x :- :int] ;;=> the notation :- means "of type"
```

▶ APP: This captures the intuition behind the application of applying an expression over another. Say you know that :concat has the following type:

```
[:concat :- [[:string :string] :>:string]
```

```
;;=> the notataion :> means the type of an application
```

That is, :concat takes a couple of expressions of the :string type and yields a result of the :string type. If you know that an expression is of the type [:string :string] type, then you know that applying :concat on it will generate an output of the :string type.

As it turns out, the previous statement sounds pretty much like a case of unification. Assume that you have to determine the type of the following expression:

```
[:app :concat [ [:app :concat [:x :y]] :z]]
```

Here, you must first find the types for `:x`, `:y`, and `:z`, the inner application of `:concat` on `:x` and `:y`, and then the type of the outer application of `:concat`. However, you probably won't be able to resolve this in that order, as you don't know when a relevant `:var` declaration will take place in the program. Besides, for every `:app` rule that you'll ever encounter, you'll have to find the type of each of its operands, and if there is a APP rule that can handle this information, you can use it to infer the type of that `:app` statement. This is actually a job where unification shines, and as you'll see in the recipe, the solution happens to be short and elegant, thanks to the very declarative nature of `core.logic`.

> For more information about Hindley-Milner, check out this paper by Luca Cardelli at `http://lucacardelli.name/Papers/BasicTypechecking.pdf`.

How to do it...

1. First of all, let's declare the facilities that we need in order to be able to use `core.logic`:

```
(ns recipe18.core
  (:require [clojure.core.logic :as logic]))
```

2. Now, we'll design a function that, given an expression, tries to use the `:var` and `:app` rules to infer new information about the expressions. This goal function is declared using the `core.logic` goal's definition operation `defne`, which brings two benefits to the table. On one hand, it allows pattern matching, which will make it very easy for us to recognize special cases and process them accordingly (with unification of the matched parts). On the other hand, `defne` operates very similar to `conde`. In this, it is able to combine the results of different cases, which is pretty much the behavior we want, as we have two overlapping pattern matching cases. The first `:app` rule is used to determine the tuple types and the second one is used to apply the APP type inference deduction. Note the use of a recursive goal in the detection of the tuple pattern, as this will help us infer the nested expression types. As our implementation is recursive, we make use of the `^:tabled` directive to tell the unification engine that this is a tabled goal. A tabled goal is a goal in which all the values for all the logical variables at stake are recorded, so it can terminate whenever `core.logic` notices a repetition of a result's patterns, guarding us from unlimited execution:

```
(logic/defne apply-rulo
  ^:tabled [e c out]
```

```
        ;; This is a tabled goal, so we ensure
        ;; termination
        ([ _ [:var x t] _] (logic/== out [x :- t]))
        ;; This recognizes a :var rules and lays out
        ;; the var "is of type" type new knowledge
        ([ _ [:app _ [x y]] _] (logic/fresh [tx ty]
                           (logic/conde
                             [(logic/membero [x :- tx] e)
                              (logic/membero [y :- ty] e)
                              (logic/== [[x y] :- [tx ty]] out)]
                             [(apply-rulo e x out)]
                             [(apply-rulo e y out)]])))
        ;; This recognizes that we are applying an expression on a
    tuple,
        ;; it infers the type of the tuple as being [:type1 :type2]
        ;; and recursively descends the tuple so nested expression
        ;; are processed too.
        ([ _ [:app e0 e1] _] (logic/fresh [ts tt]
                           (logic/membero [e0 :- [ts :> tt]] e)
                           (logic/membero [e1 :- ts] e)
                           (logic/== [[:app e0 e1] :- tt] out)))))
    ;; This is the application of the proper :app rule.
    ;; Unifies unknown vars
    ;; with any types present in the knowledge base, and applies it if
    ;; it is able to find all of the part of the :app rule.
    ;; Note the overlapping
    ;; with the previous rule, used to infer types of tuples.
```

3. In the end, we can build the function that operates a type inference in a given input environment. This function recursively processes all the members of the input environment, applies `apply-rulo` to each one of them, concatenates whatever is yielded by this operation with the environment, and recursively tries to infer more knowledge about types with the help of the new environment that is constructed. Note that we don't append a fact that is already known to the results, so we avoid divergence, that is, our environment grows indefinitely. Also note that this is a tabled goal, so its termination is ensured:

```
(def infer-typo
  (logic/tabled [e out]
                ;; This is a tabled goal to ensure
                ;; termination of the recursivity
                (logic/fresh [c r]
                  (logic/membero c e)
                  ;; we will process each one of the members
```

```
               (apply-rulo e c r)
         ;; to try to infer new facts out of it
           (logic/conde
         ;; Using a conde, we emit this new fact
             [(logic/== r out)]
         ;; plus a recursive descent
             [(logic/fresh [n]
                 (logic/nafc logic/membero  r e)
         ;; if the new fact is not already present
         ;; in the environment
                 (logic/conjo e r n)
         ;; We append it to the environment
         ;; and emit the recursive call
                 (infer-typo n out))]))))))
```

4. That's it! Let's see our type inferencer in action. Input the following code in to your REPL:

```
(logic/run* [q]  (infer-typo
                 [[:app :concat [[:app :concat  [:x :z]]
                                 [:app :concat [:y :t]]]]
                 [:var :x :string]
                 [:var :z :string]
                 [:var :y :string]
                 [:var :t :string]
                 [:concat :- [[:string :string] :> :string]]]  q))
```

5. Give it some time for execution, as the engine will have to explore a set of possible substitutions, all recursively. Eventually, you'd have:

```
([:x :- :string]
 [:z :- :string]
 [:y :- :string]
 [:t :- :string]
;;=> Application of the var rule
 [[:x :z] :- [:string :string]]
 [[:y :t] :- [:string :string]]
;;=> Determining  tuple types
 [[:app :concat [:x :z]] :- :string]
 [[:app :concat [:y :t]] :- :string]
;;=> Determining inner :app expressions types
 [[[:app :concat [:x :z]] [:app :concat [:y :t]]] :- [:string
:string]]
;;=> Tuple of inner :app expressions type
 [[:app :concat [[:app :concat [:x :z]] [:app :concat [:y :t]]]]
  :-
  :string]) ;;=> Type of the outer :app expression
```

Playing a round of checkers

Now, it's time to take a break and play checkers. For this recipe, we are going to implement an artificial intelligence kernel capable of analyzing a checkers board, determining, under the game rules, where to move while staying out of the reach of the opponent's attacks, and spotting the opportunity as to when it can capture some of the enemy's soldiers.

Let's go through a little refresher of the game of checkers. You and your opponent are located on a square chess board, but you are only able to move diagonally over black squares one step at a time. Also, you can only move forward. Both of you can capture an enemy piece if it is situated just one step away from one of your pieces, provided that when you jump over it following the diagonal square piece, the black square where you land is empty. If while doing so, from that new position you're in, you are able to capture another piece, you may go on.

To model the battle scene, we are going to use three sets: one set for the empty positions, one for the only piece that belongs to the checkers' solver engine, and one for the enemy's positions. To describe a particular situation, you may tell the solver what's in each of these sets, that is, which are the empty checkers squares, where the engine's piece is located, and where are its enemy's as well. As far as the items that will be put in those sets are concerned, we are going to store coordinates of positions on the checkers board. For instance, to notify that the enemy has 3 pieces, we just throw the 3 vectors representing the positions where these pieces are in the enemy's set.

The following figure explains how we will represent the different positions on a chess board of 6 squares edges. Note that for its construction, we will consider only the black squares. We are going to alternate a set of vectors that will cross even coordinates with odd coordinates and the odd ones with even ones:

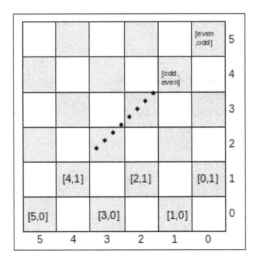

The solver is concerned about three major matters when it tries to figure out the action it must take: Which move shall he make next, will its piece be captured when it goes there? and whether it is able to capture one of the pieces of its opponent's, or more of them, if after jumping, it has the opportunity to do so. Let's see how we can implement this using `core. logic`.

How to do it...

1. For starters, we are going to declare our namespace. Note that we are using the finite domain constrains engine, `clojure.core.logic.fd`, in order to be able to derive goals where algebraic operations are involved:

```
(ns recipe19.core
  (:require [clojure.core.logic :as logic]
            [clojure.core.logic.fd :as fd]))
```

2. We will now focus on constructing the board. As mentioned earlier, we will construct a set of vectors that associate the odd x coordinates with the even y coordinates and the other way around—the even x coordinates with the odd y coordinates:

```
(defn evenso
  [size out]
  (logic/fresh [x2 se]
    (fd/in x2 (fd/interval 0  (/ size 2)))
    ;; We construct a set of integers
    ;; going from 0 to half the size
    ;; using a core.logic finite domain
    ;; facility
    (fd/* x2 2 se)
    ;; we construct the even coords
    (logic/== out se)))
    ;; and we output them by unifying them with output

(defn oddso [size out]
  (logic/fresh [x2 seo so]
    (fd/in x2 (fd/interval 0  (/  size 2)))
    ;; Same logic applies for odd part
    (fd/* x2 2 seo)
    ;; We generate an even number
    (fd/+ seo 1 so)
    ;; Then we add 1 to it
    (fd/<= so size)
    ;; We ensure that we do not exceed
```

```
;; size
   (logic/== out so)))
;; And we unify with output

(defn boardo [size out]
  (logic/fresh [e o]
    (oddso size o)
    (evenso  size e)
     ;; Then starting from even and odd numbers
    (logic/conde
     [(logic/== out [e o])]
     ;; We combine a first set of vectors
     ;; Crossing [even odd]
     [(logic/== out [o e])]))))
     ;; And crossing [odd even]
```

3. Let's build the goal function that determines where our piece will go, starting from the current position. This moves our piece up, incrementing the y part of the coordinates. You can go to the left and right by adding or subtracting 1 from the x coordinate of the set of coordinates:

```
(defn where-to-movo
  [empty cur-pos out]
  (logic/fresh [->x ->y curx cury]
    (logic/== [curx cury] cur-pos)
    ;; We destructure the position into
    ;; x and y parts
    (logic/conde
     [(fd/+ 1 curx ->x)]
     [(fd/- curx 1 ->x)])
    ;; We go left or right,
    ;; adding or substracting 1
    ;; to x and storing it into ->x
    (fd/+ cury 1 ->y)
    ;; We can only move up, adding 1 to y
    ;; and storing it into ->y
    (logic/membero [->x ->y] empty)
    ;; We verify that the target position
    ;; is empty by seeing if it is present
    ;; in the empty set
    (logic/== out [->x ->y]))))
    ;; And we unify with the output
```

4. After the solver has determined where it can move its piece, it needs a goal function that judges whether at that position, a certain piece won't be captured by any of the opponent's pieces. That's the aim of the following goal function:

```
(defn isnt-capturedo
  [empty mypos enemy out]
  (logic/fresh [x-> y->
                    ->x
                    ->y
                    y->y
                    x->x
                    new-x
                    new-y]
    (logic/== [x-> y->] enemy)
    (logic/== [->x ->y] mypos)
    ;; We destructure enemy and our
    ;; position
    (logic/conde
      [(fd/- x-> ->x x->x)]
      [(fd/- ->x x-> x->x)])
    ;; As core.logic.fd can't handle
    ;; negative numbers, we must use
    ;; a conde so we can get the difference
    ;; between the coords, whether is enemy's x higher
    ;; than the solver's, or the other way around.
    (fd/- y-> ->y y->y)
    ;; We know that the opponent can only go down
    ;; so we are able to proceed with a single
    ;; substraction, that is the opponent's y minus the
    ;; solver's
    (logic/conde
      [(fd/== x->x 1)
      (fd/== y->y 1)
;; This enemy's piece is close enough to the solver's, let's check
;; if it can capture it.
      (logic/conda
        [(fd/> x-> ->x) (fd/- ->x 1 new-x)]
;; Where is the landing x coord had the enemy captured the
;; solver's if it is at its left?
        [(fd/< x-> ->x) (fd/+ ->x  1 new-x)])
        ;; And where would it be if it did come
        ;; feom the right?
      (fd/- ->y y->y new-y)
        ;; What would the landing position y be, after
```

```
    ;; capture of the solver's piece?
    (logic/nafc logic/membero [new-x new-y] empty)
    ;; If it is not empty, the solver's piece is
 ;; safe
    (logic/== out true)]
   [(fd/> x->x 1) (logic/== out true)]
   ;; The difference between coordinates
   ;; on the x axis is higher than 1,
   ;; This piece isn't a threat to us
   [(fd/> y->y 1) (logic/== out true)]])))
   ;; Same logic for the Y axis
```

5. Besides, our artificial checkers player needs a goal function to help spot the opportunity to capture some enemy pieces. This is a recursive process, as after jumping over the piece it captured, the checkers solver needs to check whether there is another piece that it can recapture. That's why we've built a tabled goal that ensures the termination by memorizing the different values taken by the tabled logical variables and by deciding to exit an execution whenever the same patterns are encountered again:

```
(def enemy-piece-capturo
  (logic/tabled
    ;; A tabled goal ensures that our
    ;; recursive goal terminates by
    ;; detecting recurrent patterns
    ;; among the values of the logical
    ;; variables
    [empty pos->
     enemies
     out]

  (logic/fresh [x-> y->
                    ->x
                    ->y
                  x->x
                  y->y
                  new-x
                  new-y
                  new-path]
    (logic/== [x-> y->] pos->)
    (logic/membero [->x ->y] enemies)
    ;; We destructure our piece's and
    ;; all of the enemies' positions
    (logic/conde
     [(fd/- x-> ->x x->x)]
```

```
 [(fd/- ->x x-> x->x)]])
;; As negative numbers are considered
;; as failing goals, we yield a union
;; of both cases to be sure to get a
;; difference in x->x
(fd/- ->y y-> y->y)
;; We know that this is our piece,
;; we can only go up
(logic/conde
 [(fd/> x-> ->x)(fd/- ->x 1 new-x)]
 [(fd/< x-> ->x)(fd/+ ->x  1 new-x)])
;; the new-position's x after jumping,
;; adding +1 or -1 to the captured piece's x
;; depending of whether
;; we are going right or left
(fd/+ ->y y->y new-y)
;; New y can only be the enemy's piece incremented
;; by 1 as we go always up.
(logic/membero [new-x new-y] empty)
;; This landing position must be empty
(fd/== x->x 1)
(fd/== y->y 1)
;; And we must be exactly one square away
;; from the opponent's captured piece
(logic/== new-path [:from [x-> y->]
                    :capture [->x ->y]
                    :then-> [new-x new-y]])
;; At this point we have a new path:
;; Where we started, what did we capture
;; and where we landed
(logic/conde
 [(logic/== out  new-path)]
 ;; we emit this new path,
 ;; as if we were to stop here,
 ;; this is considered a legal move.
 [(logic/fresh [np]
    (enemy-piece-capturo empty
                         [new-x new-y]
                         enemies
                         np)
    ;; And we recursively check for another possible
    ;; piece to capture, adding any new discovered
    ;; path to what we've captured so far
    (logic/conjo [new-path :then->] np out)]))))))
```

6. With all the building blocks for a checkers board analyzer ready, we can now design a goal function that plays a round combining all three matters that the engine has to look after: moving, keeping the player safe, and capturing:

```
(def play-roundo
  (logic/tabled  [empty
                  cur-pos
                  enemies
                  out]
                 ;; This is a tabled goal so we can
                 ;; avoid some redundancy in the results
                 ;; caused by the unification engine
                 (logic/fresh [new-pos
                               new-empty
                               not-captured?
                               captured-them]
                   (logic/conde
                     ;; A main conde combining two main moves:
                     ;; 1. Capturing and emitting what has been
                     ;; captured
                     [(enemy-piece-capturo empty
                                           cur-pos
                                           enemies
                                           captured-them)
                      (logic/== out captured-them)]
                     ;; 2. Moving while keeping safe.
                     [(where-to-movo empty
                                     cur-pos
                                     new-pos)
                      (logic/conjo empty cur-pos new-empty)
                      ;; After moving, the piece former position
                      ;; is empty
                      (logic/everyg  #(isnt-capturedo new-empty
                                                      new-pos
                                                      %
                                                      not-captured?) enemies)
  ;; All of the enemy's pieces must not be able to capture our piece
  ;; once it moved to its new position
                      (logic/== out [:move-> new-pos])]))))
  ;; and we emit the positions in which we are safe.
```

7. In order to be able to give some checkers puzzles to the solver, we need an initialization function that takes one set of enemies and the engine's piece and emits the right set of empty squares, that is, the whole board minus the first two sets:

```
(defn prepare-board
    [board-size enemies me]
    (let [initial-board (set  (logic/run* [q]
                              (boardo
                              board-size
                              q)))]
      ;; We generate a board of size board-size
      (into '()  (clojure.set/difference initial-board (set
                                                       (conj
                                                       enemies
                                                       me))))))
      ;; and we emit empty pieces: the whole starting set minus
      ;; enemy and "me" pieces
```

8. Here is the first puzzle. Consider the situation as depicted in the following figure:

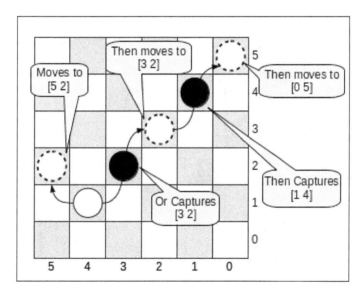

9. The solver can now safely move to the left or capture one or two pieces. Let's submit this situation to the solver by inputting the following code in to your REPL:

```
(let [enemies '([1 4] [3 2])
      me [4 1]
      empty-brd (prepare-board 8 enemies me)]
  (logic/run* [q]
    (play-roundo
      empty-brd
      me
      enemies
      q)))
;;=> ([:move-> [5 2]] ; the move
     [:from [4 1] :capture [3 2] :then-> [2 3]] ;; one capture
     [[:from [4 1] :capture [3 2] :then-> [2 3]] ;; two captures
     :then->
     [:from [2 3] :capture [1 4] :then-> [0 5]]])
```

10. Consider the following figure for the second configuration on the checkers board:

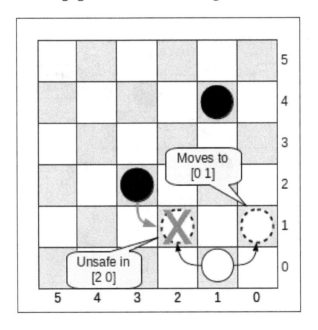

11. Although our piece can be moved to the left or right, the solver won't take the first choice, as the enemy will capture the piece at `[2 0]`. To see it run, type the following code in to the REPL:

```
(let [enemies '([3 2] [1 4])
      me [1 0]
      empty-brd (prepare-board 8 enemies me)]
  (logic/run* [q]
    (play-roundo
     empty-brd
     me
     enemies
     q)))
;;=> ([:move-> [0 1]])
```

6

Sharing by Communicating

Some problems, like those involving waiting on I/O or randomly waiting for user input, tend to be very well addressed using asynchronous programming. Asynchronous programming is a paradigm where algorithms are devised in terms of independent mini-processes that are executed concurrently and which are not synchronized using any form of locking. Those processes do share resources but are instead able to communicate through some conveyor-belt like structures called channels. In this chapter, we are going to see asynchronous programming in action using `core.async`, an implementation of this paradigm in Clojure, while developing the following recipes:

- ▶ Building a tiny web crawler
- ▶ Designing an HTML5 game
- ▶ Designing an online taxi-booking engine

Introduction

`core.async` (pretty much like the Go language, from which it draws inspiration) evolves around the concepts of co-routines and channels. A co-routine is a lightweight unit of execution, so tiny that you can literally have thousands of them in your program without worrying. These co-routines are able to communicate using channels, which act as conveyer belts: a co-routine can put an item on it or can pick one from it.

 The concepts used in `core.async` and the Go language (`http://golang.org`) are based on *Communicating Sequential Processes* by C.A.R Hoare: (`http://www.usingcsp.com/cspbook.pdf`).

`core.async` co-routines are fired by wrapping some code inside a `go` block. An invoked `go` block will return the control directly to the caller code, and its processing will be done concurrently alongside the routine that originated it in some other process (not an operating system process or a thread, but something much lighter).

Channels are created using the `chan` function or any of its variants (we'll cover some of them while elaborating on the recipes) and make it possible for code to put or to take values. As stated before, a good model to visualize what a channel is that of the conveyer belt: some routines place values in a particular channel, while some others would pick a value from it. As with physical conveyer belts, channels can be created with a maximum size (we'll then talk about buffered channels), and can be assigned a strategy to follow in case they are sent elements while they are at their full capacity . (For instance, a **dropping channel** would discard any new element arriving after it is full, and a sliding channel would drop older elements to accept new ones).

Besides the co-routines, `core.async` provides for blocking `put` and `take` operators. The blocking `put` operator would wait until there is room in the conveyor belt for the item to be placed, and the blocking `take` operator would halt the execution until there is something to be picked up from the conveyer belt. These operators can be used to create some checkpoints in a main program; for instance, it could keep blocking until a value is available to take from some channel. Blocking `put` is `>!!` and blocking `take` is `<!!` in `core.async`, are not to be confused with non-blocking `put` (`>!`) and `take` (`<!`) (with a single exclamation mark), which can only be used inside a `go` block.

In order to give some context to this description, consider the following simple `core.async` program:

```
(def ch (chan))
(go
    (>! ch (some-heavy-treatment)))
(<!! ch)
```

The first line defines a channel. By the means of a `go` block, we execute a non blocking co-routine that puts the result of `some-heavy-treatment`, once it is ready, in channel `ch`. This co-routine returns control immediately to the main program. Computation of some-heavy-treatment and putting its result in the channel are done in another process, concurrently. Now, in the main program, we wait until something lands on `ch`, by taking from it using the blocking `<!!`.

The previous program captures the essence of asynchronous programming; the co-routine initiated by the `go` block and the main program operate independently from one another, and the main program will get the result of `some-heavy-treatment` only by waiting on the value to arrive through channel `ch`.

Finally, asynchronous programming is not mainly concerned about time optimization. It is about the concurrent design using routines that handle each load of work independently and hand the result over to other processes via channels, once ready.

 For a more elaborate discussion about the difference between concurrency and parallelism, refer to this talk by Rob Pike, one of the creators of the Go language: `http://blog.golang.org/concurrency-is-not-parallelism`.

We will grasp the concepts of asynchronous programming while we work our way through the recipes in this chapter.

- **Building a tiny web crawler**: We'll design a web spider that will use `core.async` to concurrently scrape web pages in order to recursively find the links they lead to. We'll see how an asynchronous version of the web spider performs against a normal sequential one.

- **Designing an HTML5 game**: For this recipe, we will build a tiny game in `ClojureScript`. Using `core.async`, we are going to fire several UI processes that will communicate through channels, making an HTML5 game in which you have to catch balls with a bucket.

- **Designing an online taxi-booking engine**: Here we'll construct a facility to allow users to book taxis. They'll make orders through a booking central. Customers, taxis and booking-central are all modelized using `go` blocks which communicate through `core.async` channels.

Building a tiny web crawler

Let's crawl the web! For this recipe, we'll devise a little spider that'll look over webpages, searching for hyperlinks, and crawl them again for any other web pointers they happen to hold. It'll carry on with this process over and over again, recursively discovering more links, until the maximum depth of search is reached.

The crawler's job can incur exponential time usage as, for every single page, it'll have to initiate as many HTTP connections as hyperlinks it might be able to discover. If it had to do this sequentially, the overall time taken by the operation of crawling many levels of web indirections as it will have to explore only a single link at every step would be equal to the sum of the time it takes to process every single weblink, which would be quite high. That's why considering a concurrent approach might be the right approach in our case.

As it turns out, the web crawler deals with a host of slow internet connections, and that's a perfect fit for `core.async`. So our spider will proceed recursively: at each step, it will have to jump to each location, scrape it for all `href` tags, and launch as many asynchronous `http` requests as needed to crawl the links these `href` tags point to, in order to get more hyperlinks. Then, it will wait for these concurrent requests to return their own set of links, so it can record them as the result of that particular step. It carries on with that process until it reaches the requested maximum level of depth, that is, the number of steps we want the web crawler to not exceed while it drills the web for hyperlinks.

Let's see how we can implement such a web crawler. We will devise two versions, a sequential and a concurrent one, so we can compare their performances.

How to do it...

1. Let's declare the `ns` (namespace) containing the libraries we are going to use for our recipe:

```
(ns recipe20.core
  (:require [pl.danieljanus.tagsoup :as http-parser]
            [clojure.core.async :as async :refer :all :exclude
[into]]
            [clojure.zip :as z]))
```

2. We'll need a utility function that'll translate relative paths into complete URLs with absolute paths:

```
(defn fq-url
  [domain url]
  (let [protocol (first  (clojure.string/split url #"/"))]
    ;; Find the first of the tokens separated
    ;; by / in the given url.
    (if (not (some #{protocol} ["https:" "http:" "mailto:"]))
    ;; if it's not https, http or mailto
      (str domain "/" url)
    ;; append domain to it
      url))) ;; else return it as is.
```

3. Now we'll build a function that, given a target path, returns the hyperlinks contained in the web page pointed to by the last item it contains. A target path is a vector containing two URLs, [url1 url2], and is there to signal that url2 has been pointed to by url1. Note that we use a zipper to walk the `html-tree` structure generated by the parser library, `clj-tagsoup`. This library generates tags as vectors, containing properties laid out as maps and any other child tags (as vectors, obviously). For instance, `<a href="some-link">` would be parsed as `[a {:href "some-link"}`, hence the structure of our zipper. More on this in the code. Note also that we catch exceptions on HTTP connection errors so that our web spider isn't stopped later on, for instance by an unfortunate 404 error:

```clojure
(defn scrape-target-for-hrefs
  [target-path]
  (let [target (last target-path)
    ;; Target path is a vector containing [url-source url-target]
    ;; we are going to parse the second part of it, url-target
        html-tree (try  (http-parser/parse target) (catch
Exception e nil))
;; We safely parse this URL, guarding ourselves
;; from http errors
        zpr (z/zipper vector? #(filter vector? %) conj html-tree)
;; Provided that the parse tree is of the form
;; [:tag {:property1 "XYZ"}]
;; The zipper will have the following constructor functions:
;; 1. We now that the branch? function is a vector?,
;; that is, a function
;;    that tells if a particular node can have children
;;  2. The children function is one who return
;; only a seq vector elements
;; and the make-node function is simply conj, as to make a branch
;; 3. With children you must just conj vectors
;; inside another vector
        url (java.net.URL. target)
        domain (.getHost  url)
        protocol (.getProtocol url)
        ;; Using a Java URL object
        ;; we collect several information about
        ;; the url
        fqd (str protocol "://" domain)]
    (loop [output #{}
          loc (-> zpr z/down)]
      ;; We initiate the recursive
      ;; descent into the zipper
      ;; used to walk the html-tree
      (if (nil? loc)
        nil ;; if loc is nil?
            ;; html-tree must not have
            ;; been constructed due to a
            ;; http exception
            ;; Else, loc is not nil
        (if (z/end? loc)
          output ;; end of the walk, return output
          (let [tag (get (z/node loc) 0)
                a-href (get-in (z/node loc) [1 :href] )
                ;; get the current tag and if any,
                ;; a :href property inside the properties
                ;; map, that comes in the second position
```

```
                              ;; (1) in the node vector
                        new-output (if (and (= tag :a)
                                            (not (nil? a-href)))
                            ;; if it is [a {:href ...}
                                        (conj output [target (fq-url fqd
    a-href)])
                            ;; add this href, well formatted, into output
                                    output)]
                            ;; else return same thing
                        (recur new-output
                            (z/next loc))))))))))
```

```
;; and recur to the next node in the zipper
```

4. Now we will encode a sequential step. For a set of given URLs, it accesses these one after another, grabs the `href` tags they contain, and returns the whole discovered set of links:

```
(defn scrape-targets
  [targets]
    (loop [remaining-t targets
           output #{}]
      ;; loop through the targets
      ;; one after the other
      (if (not (seq remaining-t))
        output;; we are done; return result
        (let [new-ts (scrape-target-for-hrefs (first
remaining-t))]
          ;; Get the hrefs in this current target
          ;; and recur over the rest, appending them
          ;; to the final output
          (recur (rest remaining-t)
                 (concat output new-ts))))))
```

5. After that, we'll encode the concurrent step using `core.logic`. For each link in the input set, we launch a `go` block that invokes `scrape-target-for-hrefs` and stores its result in a channel. Then we collect all of the resulting `href` sets out of that channel as a global output for that particular step. Note the use of a `timeout` channel, one that expires after a given time by becoming closed. (A closed channel is one from which it is not possible to write, returning `nil` if one attempts to do so.) We used a `timeout` channel so that we do not have to wait indefinitely for a too-slow connection. We also define a helper partial version of this function, one which does the asynchronous job using channels with timeouts of 10 seconds:

```
(defn async-scrape-targets
  [ch-timeout targets]
```

```
(let [c (timeout ch-timeout)]
  ;; We use a timeout channel so
  ;; we avoid to wait undefinitely
  ;; for slow connections
  (doseq [t targets]
    ;; for each target
    (go  (>! c (scrape-target-for-hrefs t))))
  ;; launch a co-routine that asynchronously launches
  ;; a scraping operation and puts the results, once they're
  ;; ready, into the channel
  (loop [cur-t 0
         output #{}]
    ;; we loop as many times
    ;; as the number of targets
    (if (= cur-t (count targets))
      output ;; end of the looping, we
             ;; return output
      (let [new-ts (<!! c)]
        ;; every time, wait for something new from
        ;; the channel, and when it lands, recur
        ;; to wait for the next one
        (recur (inc cur-t)
               (concat output new-ts)))))))

;; a helper function scraping targets with a 10s timeout
(def async-scrape-targets-10s (partial async-scrape-targets
10000))
```

6. Finally, we can write `run-spider`, which will scrape newly discovered links for as many times as is set as the value of `max-depth`, recursively discovering more and more links. We parameterized it with `scrapte-target-fn`, so we can use either one of our implementations: the sequential one or the asynchronous one:

```
(defn run-spider
  [start max-depth scrape-target-fn]
  ;; We loop beginning by a first scraping
  ;; of our starting set of target paths,
  (loop [targets (scrape-target-fn start)
         output #{}
         cur-depth 0]
    (if (= cur-depth max-depth)
      output
;; if we reached max-depth, we return output
      (let [new-targets (scrape-target-fn targets)]
;; else we scrape again what we just
```

```
;; discovered, appending them to the result
;; and incrementing current level of depth
;; so we can end the recursion.
(recur new-targets
       (into  output new-targets)
       (inc cur-depth))))))
```

7. Now we'll benchmark the two versions. We'll clock each one of them for a maximum depth of 1, starting from a certain website (and using a wireless residential broadband connection):

```
(time (count (run-spider [["http://www.clojure.tn"]]
1 scrape-targets )))
;;"Elapsed time: 27416.338574 msecs"
;; => 462
(time (count (run-spider [["http://www.clojure.tn"]]
 1 async-scrape-targets-10s )))
"Elapsed time: 11781.256674 msecs"
;; => 462
```

The concurrent version, in this case, is able to finish its job in half the time it took the sequential one. Nevertheless, be aware that these results may vary for larger depths as network conditions may cause substantial noise that could affect the benchmarking.

Designing an HTML5 game

Thinking about games in general leads you to design a rather complex system in which you'd have several independent entities interacting on the playing board. This seems to be a perfect case for `core.async`, especially considering how plain JavaScript code could have become bloated had you gone the classical way: laying out a solution inside a single huge loop. In fact, `core.async` and `ClojureScript` will enable us to design a very elegant and human-readable solution, one considering every element of the UI as an independent co-routine, executing concurrently and communicating through channels.

Imagine that you want to design a very simple game in which balls are falling from the sky and you must catch as many of them as you can with your bucket. But beware: if a single ball hits the floor, the game is over. Each time you are able to catch a ball, your score increases.

Out of these requirements, we can detect several processes that we'd have to build in order to give birth to our game:

- **The balls process**: This is to throw the balls from the roof all the way down to the floor.

- **The bucket process**: You'll need it to capture your mouse movement and translate it into your bucket's position.

▶ **The painting processes**: These will draw the balls and the bucket onto the screen.

▶ **The game rules engine**: This will enforce the game rules, basically increasing score if the balls fall into the bucket or resetting it otherwise, while giving the player one "game over" alert.

▶ **The master process**: fires all of the other processes, and ensures communication between them by multiplexing the different messages they are exchanging. The master process also maintains the state of the game: the positions of the balls and bucket as well as the current player's score.

Let's see how `core.async` will help us assemble the ball-catcher game!

How to do it...

1. First of all, you'll have to set up your development environment so that you can enjoy an interactive REPL-based workflow for ClojureScript. For that, one simple approach would be to use Figwheel, which you can read about here: `https://github.com/bhauman/lein-figwheel`.

2. You'll also need one HTML page in order to see our game as it is being constructed. In that HTML page, you'll use an HTML5 canvas to draw the graphical environment and an `h3` header to show the score to the player. Note that our ClojureScript target is `main.js`. It will host the dynamic REPL-based development environment, making your work seamlessly available in the browser for you to test. Please read through the Figwheel documentation to be aware of the different compilation options needed to have your program compiled into that file. Here is the HTML page `index.html`:

 You'll have to access the `index.html` file from the file system just as you would do for a regular local document (by double-clicking it or opening it in a browser).

```
<!DOCTYPE html>
<html>
  <head></head>
  <body>
    <table height="100%" width="100%">
      <tr>
       <td width="400vw"></td>
       <td witdh="500vw"  style=" margin:0; padding:0;" >
    <h2>Your Score:</h2>
    <h3 id="score">0</h3>
    <canvas   id="playboard"
       width="400vw"
       height="500vh"
       style="border:1px solid black;">
```

```
        </canvas>
          </td>
          <td width="400vw"></td>
        </tr>
        </table>
        <script src="main.js" type="text/javascript"></script>
      </body>
    </html>
```

3. Inside our main ClojureScript program, let's define our `ns` (namespace) so we can use `core.async` facilities for this platform:

```
(ns recipe21.core
  (:require [cljs.core.async :as async :refer [<! >! chan alts!]])
  (:require-macros [cljs.core.async.macros :refer [go]]))
```

4. We'll start by working on the ball process. In our recipe, a ball will have discrete coordinates, that is, a position describing which portion of the play-board it is in. If we divide the board into a grid by splitting the horizontal and vertical axes into x-size and y-size parts, respectively, we'll mean by a "ball's position" the particular square on that grid it is sitting on. Later on, we'll need to translate these coordinates into actual positions on the screen while rendering the game to the player. For now, we'll use this system to conveniently move the balls across the grid and verify the game's rules.

5. Let's build two utility functions beforehand. The first one yields a starting position for a ball, such as "x is holding a random number less than x-size and y is set to zero", so as to locate that ball into some random position on the roof. The second utility function will make the ball fall, increasing its y coordinate by 1 when called:

```
(defn starting-ball-pos
  [x-size]
  [(.floor js/Math
            (* (dec x-size)
               (.random js/Math)))
   ;; A random position for x
   0])
   ;; Starting from the Top setting y at 0

(defn ball-fall
  [coords]
  [(get coords 0)
   ;; Same X component
   (inc (get coords 1))])
   ;; and increasing Y by 1
```

6. Next we build the balls co-routine. This co-routine is going to make balls rain; starting from the top, it begins by making a ball drop until it hits the floor and resumes from the roof all over again. It works by calling `ball-fall` recursively, after some sleeping delay. This mechanism controls the rate at which the balls are dropped. The positions are sent through a channel so the game master process can process them.

```
(defn balls
  ([x-size
    y-size
    b->m
    step-duration
    coords]
   ;; this Arity is for recursive call.
   (go
     (let [[cur-x cur-y] coords
           ;; If the balls hits the floor
           new-coords (if (= cur-y
                            (dec y-size))
                        (starting-ball-pos x-size)
           ;; start over from the roof
                        (ball-fall coords))]
       ;; else make the ball fall
       (>! b->m new-coords)
       ;; and put the new position
       ;; into a channel
       (js/setTimeout
        ;; and after step-duratin
        #(balls x-size y-size
                b->m
                step-duration
                new-coords)
        ;; do it once again
        step-duration))))
  ;; This arity is for first time calling
  ([x-size
    y-size
    b->m
    step-duration]
   (balls x-size
          y-size
          b->m
          step-duration
          (starting-ball-pos x-size))))
```

7. Now we focus on the bucket process. The bucket responds to our mouse moves on the canvas, so we will have to assign to its `onmousemove` event handler a function that is able to determine the pointer coordinates when this event is fired and then send them through a channel to the master game process. Note that these coordinates are absolute, and as we'll be rendering the bucket on a canvas, we'll have to offset them by its dimensions, but more on this in a minute:

```
(defn get-mouse-coords
    ;; the function that will be
    ;; assigned to the canvas onmousemove
    [m->m e]
    ;; the channel is put on the first
    ;; position in the arguments list
    ;; as we'll attach a partial
    ;; function where the channel is bound and
    ;; which is having just the event as
    ;; argument to the onmousemove event
    (go   (>! m->m
              [(.-clientX e)
               (.-clientY e)]))))
    ;; we send the coords of this
    ;; onmousemove event through a channel

(defn bucket
    [canvas
     m->m]
    (set! (.-onmousemove canvas)
          ;; we attach the previously
          ;; developed function to the
          ;; playboard (canvas) onmousmove
          ;; event
          (partial get-mouse-coords
                   m->m)))
```

8. As far as rendering the play-board on the screen is concerned, here we develop three functions, one that clears the HTML5 canvas and two that draw the ball and the bucket individually:

```
(defn clear-playboard!
    [canvas]
    (let [context (.getContext canvas "2d")]
        ;; we get the graphical context
        ;; of the canvas and we clear the
        ;; rectangle that spans all over it
        (.clearRect context
                    0
```

```
                            0
                            (.-width canvas)
                            (.-height canvas)))))

(defn paint-ball!
  [canvas
   x
   y
   y-size]
  (let [context (.getContext canvas "2d")
        ;; we get the graphical context of the canvas
        play-board-height (.-height canvas)
        ;; its height
        ball-height (.floor js/Math
                            (/ play-board-height y-size))
        ;; the ball height is the size
        ;; of one square on the virtual grid
        ;; we are considering the canvas to be
        ball-center-x (*  (+ x 0.5)
                          ball-height)
        ;; the X position of the center of the ball
        ball-center-y (* (+ y 0.5)
                          ball-height)
        ;; the Y position
        ball-radius (/ ball-height 2)]
        ;; and the Radius, being the half of
        ;; the ball height
    (.beginPath context)
        ;; we initiate drawing in the context
    (.arc context
          ball-center-x
          ball-center-y
          ball-radius 0
          (* 2 (.-PI js/Math)) false )
    ;; we draw a full arc
    (set! (.-fillStyle context)
          "orange")
    (.fill context)
    ;; we fill it in orange
    (set! (.-lineWidth context) 5)
    (set! (.-strokeStyle context)
          "#003300")
    (.stroke context)))
```

```
                 ;; and we draw a border around it

       (defn paint-bucket!
         [canvas
          x
          x-size]
         (let [context (.getContext canvas "2d")
                 ;; we get the graphical context of the
                 ;; canvas
                 rect (.getBoundingClientRect canvas)
                 ;; we get the coords of the bounding
                 ;; rectangle of the canvas so we can
                 ;; translate absolute coordinates
                 ;; into coordinates relative to the canvas
                 x-start (- x  (.-left rect))
                 ;; x on the canvas
                 play-board-width (.-width canvas)
                 bucket-width (.floor js/Math
                                      (* 1.5
                                         (/ play-board-width x-size)))
                 ;; the bucket width is one time and a half
                 ;; one square on the canvas virtual grid
                 bucket-height (* bucket-width 0.75)
                 ;; bucket made thin this way

                 y (- (.-height canvas)
                      bucket-height)]
                 ;; y, or where to put the higher-left
                 ;; corner of the bucket
           (do
             (.beginPath context)
             ;; We initiate drawing on the canvas
             (.rect context
                    x-start
                    y
                    bucket-width
                    bucket-height)
             (set!   (.-fillStyle context)
                     "yellow")
             (.fill context)
             ;; we draw the bucket
             (set!   (.-lineWidth context ) 7)
             (set! (.-strokeStyle context)
                   "black")
```

```
      (.stroke context)))))
    ;; and we draw a border around it
```

9. Time to devise the game logic engine, along with a score maintaining process. If the ball reaches the floor and happens to land in the bucket, we send some information to a score maintaining process, through a channel, in order to increase our points. If instead it falls on the ground, the game rules engine sends a "game over" signal to the co-routine that manages the scores, so it is reset to 0:

```
(defn check-game-rules
  [canvas
   x-size
   y-size
   ball-coords
   bucket-coords
   m->g]
  (let [[center-ball-x center-ball-y] ball-coords
        [cur-bucket-x _] bucket-coords
        play-board-height (.-height canvas)
        ball-height (.floor js/Math
                            (/ play-board-height y-size))
        context (.getContext canvas "2d")
        rect (.getBoundingClientRect canvas)
        real-bucket-x (- cur-bucket-x
                         (.-left rect))
        real-ball-center-x (+
                             (* (+ center-ball-x 0.5)
                                ball-height)
                             (.-left rect))
        play-board-width (.-width canvas)
        bucket-width (.floor js/Math
                            (* 1.5
                               (/ play-board-width x-size)))]
    ;; geometrical information is computed about the ball
    ;; and the bucket, just like in painting them
    (go
      (if (= center-ball-y (dec y-size))
        ;; If the ball reaches the floor
        (if (and (<= real-ball-center-x
                     (+ cur-bucket-x bucket-width))
                 (>= real-ball-center-x
                     cur-bucket-x))
          ;; and its center is "in the bucket"
          (>! m->g :add)
          ;; we send :add to the score maintaining process
```

```
                    (>! m->g :lost))))))
                 ;; else we send a :lost signal

        (defn update-score!
          ;; The score maintaining process
          [score-place
           score
           m->g]
          (go
            (while true
              (let [msg (<! m->g)]
                ;; If a signal is received from the game-rules-engine
                (cond
                   (= msg :add)(set! (.-innerHTML score-place)
                                     (swap! score inc))
                   ;; if it was :add, we add 1 to the atom maintaining
                   ;; score state, and we show it on the page
                   (= msg :lost)(do
                                   ;; else, we notify the player
                                   (js/alert "Game Over!")
                                   ;; and we set the score to 0
                                   ;; initiating a new game
                                   (set! (.-innerHTML score-place)
                                        (reset! score 0)))))))))
```

10. Finally, we can put all of the pieces together inside the `master!` process. This main procedure will call all of the game processes. It will maintain the state of the ball, the bucket, and the score, while making sure the game rules engine checks that no balls have hit the floor without landing in your bucket. Here it is:

```
    (defn master!
     [x-size
      y-size
      step-duration]
     (let [canvas (.getElementById js/document
                                    "playboard")
            score-place (.getElementById js/document
                                          "score")
            ;; We grab the UI elements we are going
            ;; to manipulate, the canvas for the play-board,
            ;; and the h3 header for showing the score
            b->m (chan) ;; a channel from the ball to the master
            m->m (chan) ;; a channel from the mouse to the master
            m->g (chan) ;; a channel from the game-rule-engine to
                        ;; the score-updating engine
```

```
       ball-coords (atom [])    ;; to keep state of the ball
       bucket-coords (atom []) ;; to keep state of the bucket
       score (atom 0)            ;; to keep state of the score
       _ (balls x-size y-size b->m step-duration)
       ;; we launch the balls co-routine
       _ (bucket canvas m->m)
       ;; we launch the bucket co-routine
       _ (update-score! score-place score m->g)]
       ;; we launch the score maintaining co-routine
  (go
    (while true
      (let [[msg ch] (alts! [b->m m->m])]
        ;; Whenever a message arrives from mouse
        ;; or from the ball co-routine
        (clear-playboard! canvas)
        ;; clear the canvas, we are going
        ;; to repaint a new situation
        (cond
          (= ch b->m) (do
                  ;;if it is from the mouse
                      (reset! ball-coords msg)
                ;; update the balls coords state
                      (check-game-rules canvas
                                        x-size
                                        y-size
                                        @ball-coords
                                        @bucket-coords
                                        m->g))
                    ;; and summon the rules checker
          (= ch m->m) (reset! bucket-coords msg))
                       ;; if it is from the bucket
                       ;; update the bucket state
        (paint-ball! canvas
                    (get @ball-coords 0)
                    (get @ball-coords 1)
                    y-size)
        ;; paint the ball at the new coords
        (paint-bucket! canvas
                    (get @bucket-coords 0)
                    x-size))))))
        ;; paint the bucket at the new coords
```

11. And that's it! Launch the master process at your Figwheel REPL. The grid of the game will be set to the size 7 by 7, and we'll set the ball speed to fall by one grid square every 200 milliseconds. Make sure that you loaded `index.html` in your browser:

```
(master! 7 7 200)
```

You will see balls randomly dropping from the sky. Make sure you catch them all!

Designing an online taxi-booking engine

Asynchronous programming is a very good choice for making independent processes collaborate, relieving the designer from the burden of maintaining a global state for all of the entities at stake. We are going to showcase this in a recipe, in which we will simulate an online taxi-booking engine.

In the system we are longing to build, no global state will be maintained. Instead, we are going to fire as many processes as we have taxis, and a couple more to ensure that the collaboration between them occurs properly. Finally, customer requests will land in our system from the outer world via channels.

The rules our taxi-booking engine obeys will be kept as simple as possible a given taxi, whose status is initially `:free`, keeps moving randomly around town unless it receives from headquarters a customer request that matches the place it happens to be in at that particular moment. Then, it notifies headquarters that it is willing to process that particular request and sets its status to `:booked`. Once it is booked, a taxi does not move any more and cannot accept any other request (even matching its current location) until it is sent a `:confirm` message by headquarters, thus making it move to the request destination and eventually setting it to `:free`. It may also be responded to with a `:release` message, which immediately sets it to `:free` to convey that the request it is waiting on is no longer valid.

At their end, headquarters spends time accepting customer requests and maintaining a state of such pending requests accordingly. Once they send `:request` messages to taxis, they wait on their responses. They assign the job to the first taxi that acknowledges its readiness with a `:booking` message, by sending that particular driver a `:confirm` message. In the meantime they consider that job done and delete that customer request from the queue they are using to keep track of pending customer inquiries. After that, any other taxi that responds with a `:booked` notification for that query will be sent a `:release` message so that it can be set to `:free` again and made ready to process other requests.

`core.async` allows us to come up with a solution in which no shared global state between those different entities is maintained: each taxi will maintain its own, whereas headquarters will only care about following customer requests. This recipe showcases particularly well the spirit behind this chapter's name: sharing by communicating!

How to do it...

1. Let's, for starters, import the Clojure facilities that we are going to put to use in our program:

```
(ns recipe22.core
   (:require  [clojure.core.async :as async
                :refer :all
                :exclude [merge into]]))
```

2. We'll need a tiny function to make it possible for our taxis to randomly pick a town and go visit it if they have nothing else to do:

```
(defn pick-a-town
   [towns]
   (get towns (rand-int (count towns))))
```

3. Now let's design our `taxi!` function. This function launches the co-routine that spends its time waiting on requests from headquarters, setting its state with respect to the signals it is sent from them. It also notifies headquarters about its will to carry out a job that pleases, that is, a customer request whose departure town happens to be the same at the town it is currently in. Once it sets itself `:booked`, a taxi will not accept any other requests and it will not be allowed to carry on with its random town visits. Note that taxis don't wait indefinitely in a particular position; we made them listen for requests arriving from `timeout` channels that will eventually be closed after a predefined period of time. If no customer request arrives before these channels expire, the taxis move to another random town. This mechanism ensures that no deadlock is met in our system if no taxi happens to be in the right town for a particular request:

```
(defn taxi!
  [taxi-id
   t->m  ;; A channel from taxi to headquarters
   m->t
    towns
    time-to-towns]
;; A channel from headquarters to taxis
  (let [max-waiting (timeout 3000)
;; A timeout channel to cap a taxi's wait in a particular town
        my-state (atom {:status :free :at (pick-a-town towns)})]
;; Setting initial state for a taxi; :free at a random town
    (go
      (while true
;; Launching the co-routine
        (let [[v c] (alts! [m->t max-waiting])]
          ;; Wait for a message on headquarters
          ;; or Quit if timeout is reached
```

```
(cond
  (and v
;; a message arrived, we are not here after a timeout
        (= (get @my-state :at) (get v :from))
;; The town in the request is the one
;; the taxi is currently in
        (= (get v :type) :request)
        ;; this is a request
        (= (:status @my-state) :free))
  ;;And the taxi is free
                    (let [customer (get v :customer)
                    taxi-currently-at (get @my-state :at)
                  customer-currently-at  (get v :from)
                        destination (get v :to)]
                    (>! t->m {:taxi-id taxi-id
                        :state (reset! my-state
                            {:status :booked
                             :customer customer
                             :at taxi-currently-at
                             :to destination})})))
;; send the :booked message to headquarters
          (and v
              (= (get v :type) :release)) (swap! my-state
                                    merge
                              {:status :free})
;; If the taxi receives a :release message, set him free


          (and v
;; If it receives a :confirm and it is booked
              (= (get v :type) :confirm)
(= (:status @my-state) :booked))
(let [destination (get @my-state :to)
                      customer (get @my-state :customer)]
                    (println "Taxi:" taxi-id
                  " has been confirmed for customer")
                    (Thread/sleep time-to-towns)
;; Get the customer to its destination
                          (reset! my-state
                            {:status :free
                             :at destination})
;; Change my state to :free
;; And my current-town to destination
                    (println "Taxi:" taxi-id
                      ": customer " customer
```

```
                                              "arrived to" destination))
                      ;; v is nil?. We are here after a timeout.
                      ;; If the taxi is not booked, move along
                      ;; by picking a random town and visiting it
                  (and (nil? v)
(not= (:status @my-state) :booked))
(let [new-town (pick-a-town towns)]
                                        (Thread/sleep time-to-towns)
                                             (reset! my-state
{:status :free
                                  :at new-town})))))))))
```

4. Now, given a set of channels pointing to taxis and a pending requests queue, we are going to build a co-routine that always sends all queries to all taxis:

```
(defn send-requests-to-taxis!
  [taxi-channels
   requests
   step-time]
  (go
    (do
      (while true
        (doseq [r @requests] ;; for every request
          (doseq [t taxi-channels]
            ;; for every channel to taxi
            (>! t r) ;; send that request to that taxi
            (Thread/sleep step-time))))))
        ;; and wait some time before retrying with
        ;; maybe a new requests queue?
```

5. We'll also need a co-routine that processes messages that flow from taxis, sends `:confirm` or `:release` messages to "whom it may concern", and changes the pending requests accordingly. Remember, we delete a request along with sending a `:confirm` message as we consider that our taxis are trustworthy. In real life, you might want to set up a more robust control mechanism. Note that we consider that channels from and to headquarters are actually maps, like so: `{:taxi-id #<channel>...}` Thus, we can keep track of where to send responses for whom:

```
(defn confirm-or-release-taxis!
  [m->taxis
   taxis->m
   requests]
  (go
    (while true
      (let [[v c] (alts! (into [] (vals taxis->m)))
            ;; wait for some message from the taxis.
            ;; channels are the values of the map:
```

```
;; {:taxi-id #<core-async-Channel...> ...}
response-state (get v :state)
customer-id (get response-state :customer)
taxi-id (get v :taxi-id)]
(if (= (get response-state :status) :booked )
  ;; If it is a :booked message
  ;; actually it is the only possible
  ;; kind of message but we keep it for
  ;; future evolutions
  (let [m->t (get m->taxis taxi-id)]
    ;; We get the relevant channel
    ;; so we can send the response
    ;; to the right taxi
    (if (some #{customer-id}
            (mapv :customer @requests))
      ;; If the message is about a query
      ;; still pending (present in our queue)
      (do
        (>! m->t {:type :confirm})
        ;; Confirm that taxi
        (swap! requests #(into [] (filter
                                    (fn [r]
                                    (not= (get r :customer)
                                            customer-id)))
                              %)))
        ;; And delete it from the queue. It has been
        ;; processed
      (>! m->t {:type :release})))))))))
        ;; Else, It is a response about an old
        ;; request that's no more valid. We set
        ;; this waiting taxi free.
```

6. We'll also need an interface with the outer world, one which will feed our requests queue. We set up a co-routine that does just that:

```
(defn accept-requests!
  [c->m
   requests]
  (go
    (while true
      (let [r (<! c->m)]
        ;;If something comes up
        ;;through the channel
        (swap! requests conj r)))))
        ;; Add it to our requests queue
```

7. Just before we can assemble the final function, we'll have to design a mechanism that launches co-routines for the taxis, attaching to each one the right channels from and to headquarters. Remember, channels are put in maps in the form `{:taxi-id #<core.async-channel...> ...}`, so we are able to keep track of corresponding channels and taxis:

```
(defn init-taxis!
  [taxis
   taxis->m
   m->taxis
   towns
   time-to-towns]
  (doseq [taxi-id taxis]
    ;; for each taxi
    (taxi! taxi-id
    ;; Launch a co-routine that holds that Taxi-ID
           (get taxis->m taxi-id)
           (get m->taxis taxi-id)
           towns
           time-to-towns)))
    ;; With channels from and to headquarters
    ;; referenced by this same taxi-id
```

8. And now it's time to assemble all of the components we developed in order to come up with the `hq` function, the one that launches the online taxi-booking engine:

```
(defn hq
  [c->m
   taxis
   towns
   time-to-towns]
  (let [requests (atom [])
    ;; creating an empty queue for requests
        taxis->m (zipmap taxis (repeat (chan)))
        m->taxis (zipmap taxis (repeat (chan)))]
    ;; and the channels from and to taxis
    (init-taxis! taxis taxis->m m->taxis towns time-to-towns)
    ;; we launch the taxis
    (accept-requests! c->m requests)
    ;; Accept incoming requests
    (send-requests-to-taxis! (vals m->taxis) requests 2000)
    ;; Launch the request sending co-routine
    (confirm-or-release-taxis! m->taxis taxis->m requests)))
    ;; and the confirmation or release manager
```

9. Let's help some people go home. First of all, let's create some towns and taxis:

```
(def time-to-towns 2000)

(def towns [:ariana
            :tunis
            :carthage
            :hammam-lif
            :rades
            :bardo
            :casa])

(def taxis [:t-john
            :t-bob
            :t-salah
            :t-ali
            :t-rich
            :t-dennis
            :t-steve])
```

10. Now we'll create a channel that'll transport our requests to the engine, and we'll launch it:

```
(def c->m (chan))
(hq c->m taxis towns time-to-towns)
```

11. And here's a customer waiting for a taxi to bring them home. Input the following code in your REPL:

```
(go (>! c->m  {:customer :rafik
               :from :ariana
               :to :tunis
               :type :request}))
```

12. And let's see what happens:

```
Taxi: :t-salah  has been confirmed for customer
Taxi: :t-salah : customer  :rafik arrived to :tunis
```

13. So :rafik eventually went home safely!

7

Transformations as First-class Citizens

In this chapter we are going to cover advanced techniques, taking advantage of some of Clojure's powerful tools inherent to its functional nature. We'll discuss functions as privileged language constructs in the following recipes:

- ▶ Building a recursive descent parser using trampoline
- ▶ Implementing a reusable mini-firewall using transducers
- ▶ Building a little unification engine with the continuation-passing style

Introduction

Functions in Clojure are first-class citizens. You can pass them around like ordinary parameters, store them as any other value, and even generate them programmatically. But this special and privileged position allows for more advanced algorithmic techniques, adding to the expressive power of Clojure.

Indeed, functions allow for more complex transformations that can be reusable, compoundable, and decoupled from the data structures they operate on. They can even serve as the foundation of a whole new computation paradigm, bringing more expressive power to the developer.

In this chapter, we are going to cover how transformations, as privileged language constructs, can help in addressing many algorithmic challenges like those found in exploring alternative styles for mutual recursion, piling up transducers into a reusable tiny firewall and using an alternative programming method known as continuation passing style.

> ▶ **Building a recursive descent parser using trampoline**: In this recipe we are going to use a construct that allows for efficient mutual recursion, **trampoline**, in order to build a recursive descent parser for symbolic expressions. This type of parser implements grammar rules as functions that mutually call each other, and trampolining will therefore be needed for a safe call-stack operation.

> ▶ **Implementing a reusable mini-firewall using transducers**: We'll make good use of the new Clojure 1.7 feature, **transducers**, to be able to simulate a tiny firewall operation through implementing reusable transforming units and compounding them. We'll also see how this firewall can operate on different sorts of input streams with no code change.

> ▶ **Building a little unification engine with the continuation-passing style**: For this recipe, we'll showcase an alternative programming style that uses functions as flow control elements, **continuation passing** style, in order to implement a simple symbolic expression unification engine.

Building a recursive descent parser using trampoline

A recursive descent parser, as the name implies, makes heavy use of recursion in order to process some input tokens and be able to tell if they comply with a particular grammar code. For each of the grammar rules, such a parser will have to fire a function that proceeds with the verification of the input according to this very rule.

Let's consider, for the purposes of this recipe, a very simple grammar code: one that allows describing the structure of a symbolic expression that is very broadly speaking a set of elements confined between parentheses:

```
S = sexp
sexp =  "(" element* ")"
element = term | sexp
term = [a-zA-Z0-9]*'
```

Our parser recognizes as valid structures those which are symbolic expressions, and such expressions contain a list of elements delimited by left and right parentheses. An element is either a term or a symbolic expression itself, and a term is an alphanumeric string.

You may notice the mutual recursion present in this grammar code: a `sexp` function may contain a list of `element` functions that are `sexp` functions too. Considering the nature of the parser we want to implement, which implies using functions to verify each and every rule of the grammar code, we may run into a situation where the `sexp` function calls the `element` one and element calls `sexp` as well.

Now why should we be concerned about mutual recursion at all? As it turns out, this sort of configuration where you have two functions calling each other can lead to a very high call stack usage: during execution, you exponentially store contexts and dive into new frames as you recursively call this function that, in turn, calls the other function that will do the same over and over again.

The problem of simple recursion, if you remember, was addressed by Clojure for tail calls by the `recur` construct. For remainders, recursive calls at the tail of the caller (that is, recursion done as the very last instruction of the function) lead easily to what we call tail call optimization, a technique transforming all such recursions into simple looping constructs, preventing the explosion of the call stack. There exists a similar mechanism for mutual recursion at tail positions, operating pretty much in the same manner: the `trampoline` construct.

When you launch a function with `trampoline`, if its result is a function it will be launched in turn. If that yields a function too, it will also be fired. This logic will be maintained as long as the functions launched return functions themselves, until one particular iteration yields a value, at which point `trampoline` will return it. How does this relate to tail call optimization? Internally, `trampoline` uses `recur` to launch the resulting function, from a tail position, transforming all of these generated calls into plain loops. To better understand this, have a look at the implementation of the `trampoline` function in Clojure:

```clojure
(defn trampoline
  "trampoline can be used to convert algorithms requiring mutual
   recursion without stack consumption. Calls f with supplied args, if
   any. If f returns a fn, calls that fn with no arguments, and
   continues to repeat, until the return value is not a fn, then
   returns that non-fn value. Note that if you want to return a fn as a
   final value, you must wrap it in some data structure and unpack it
   after trampoline returns."
  {:added "1.0"
   :static true}
  ([f]
     (let [ret (f)]
       (if (fn? ret)
         (recur ret)
         ret)))
  ([f & args]
     (trampoline #(apply f args))))
```

Note how recur behaves if the result of firing the function f yields a function too (which is tested using fn? Predicate) : it recurs handing the resulting function over to the new recursive iteration, ensuring that "trampolined" calls are processed as loops, which is way gentler to the call stack. Hence, mutual recursion is efficiently handled by writing the different callers in such a way that whenever a call needs to be made, the very function that needs to be fired is returned. Whenever you need to end the recursion, you only need to return a value. Let's see this mechanism in detail while implementing our parser.

How to do it...

1. Let's declare our namespace. Nothing fancy here as no library will be imported.

   ```
   (ns recipe23.core)
   ```

2. We'll need an atom holding the tokens we are going to run our parser into. This is to be seen as the state of our parse operation. Whenever a symbol is accepted as per the grammar rules, it gets consumed and removed from that atom. A successful parse operation means necessarily an empty token sequence, but an empty sequence may not necessarily mean that we ran into no problems. Indeed, we can terminate the parse while still needing to consume closing parenthesis, for instance:

   ```
   (def symbols (atom []))
   ```

3. Let's define a function that consumes a token from the symbols sequence. This simply sets the global symbols atom to its rest:

   ```
   (defn next-symbol!
     []
     (swap! symbols rest))
   ```

4. Now we'll implement accept!, a function that tests whether the provided symbol corresponds to the one currently present at the head of the symbols atom. If the symbol is accepted, we move forward by one position in our symbols atom, holding the state of the parser. This function will be used whenever we need to verify that the symbol we have at any particular moment conforms to what should be there, according to the grammar code. We can also use multiple accept! calls as a switch that help us determine which rule to explore in our grammar, but more of this in a few moments:

   ```
   (defn accept!
     [re-s]
     (if-let [current-symbol (first @symbols)]
       ;; symbols is not empty
       (do
         (if (re-matches (re-pattern re-s)
                         current-symbol)
   ;; If the symbol if equal to what we are expecting
   ```

```
(do
  (next-symbol!)
  ;; Move to the next symbol
  true)
  ;; and return true, we accept it.
  false)) ;; Else we discard it, not moving to
          ;; next symbol
  false))      ;; symbols is empty, nothing to accept.
```

5. It's now time to define the function implementing the `term` rule. This is simply done by accepting an element falling under the set of expressions conforming to the given regular expression:

```
(def term (partial accept! "[a-zA-Z0-9]*"))
```

6. Let's reflect upon the mutual callers that are the `elements!` and `sexp!` functions, implementing the corresponding grammar rules. First, as you'll definitely implement one function before the other, you will have to declare the one being called from that as being implemented first, so the compiler can recognize it at that point. Second, as `elements!` is a recursive call as well, it is in fact recognizing an arbitrary list of terms or symbolic expressions you'll need to trampoline it from the `sexp!` function too, so it can be efficiently handled. Here is the implementation:

```
(declare elements!)
;; We declare elements! as it will be used in sexp!
;; before its actual implementation

(defn sexp!
  []
  (cond
;; Verify if we are at an opening parenthesis
    (accept! "\\(") (do
                      (trampoline elements!)
;; recursively verify the elements
                      (if (accept! "\\)")
;; and verify if we have a closing parenthesis
                        elements!
;; then carry on with other elements
                        (println "Parse Error!")))
;; else emit a parse error for a non-present closing parenthesis
    :default nil))
;; Return nil else, mainly to terminate recursion in the case
;; the symbols atom gets empty.

(defn elements!
  []
```

```
(cond
  (term)   elements! ;; if we accept a term, recur
  :default sexp!))

;; else, try to see if it is a symbolic expression
```

7. Finally, we'll build `parse-sexp`. This function will trampoline `sexp!` as the first rule of our grammar says. To be able to tell if the parsing has been successful, we are going to test the emptiness of the `symbols` atom:

```
(defn parse-sexp
  [a-sexp]
  (do
    (reset! symbols a-sexp)
    ;; Init the symbols atom with the succession
    ;; of tokens given as a parameter
    (trampoline sexp!)
    ;; trampoline sexp!
    (if (not-empty @symbols)
      (println "Parse Error!"))))
    ;; issue a parse error if the symbols
    ;; were not totally consumed
```

8. And that's it for the implementation! Let's see our parser in action. Define the following symbolic expressions:

```
(def sample-sexp1 ["("
                     "(" "a" "c" ")" ")"])
(def sample-sexp2 ["("
                     "(" "a" "c" ")"
                     "d" ")" ")"])
(def sample-sexp3 ["("
                     "(" "+" "c" ")"
                     ")" ")"])
```

9. The first one is lacking a closing parenthesis and shall not pass. The second one is totally fine, and the third one presents a symbol not recognized by our grammar definition. Let's see how our parser performs:

```
(parse-sexp sample-sexp1)
Parse Error!
;; => nil
  (parse-sexp sample-sexp2)
;; => nil
(parse-sexp sample-sexp3)
Parse Error!
Parse Error!
Parse Error!
;; => nil
```

Implementing a reusable mini-firewall using transducers

Clojure's unique way of describing data transformations, reminiscent of its Lisp and functional heritage, has set a new standard in the art of designing highly expressive algorithms.

Clojure makes you address your problems in terms of highly declarative multi-stage transformations, and more often than not, you'll find your self alternating `map`, `reduce`, `filter`, and likely operations on the powerful `seq` abstraction to express the solution you came with as if you were explaining it in plain English to some non IT-savvy person. This declarative way of thinking yields much expressive power, and just looking at how SQL is ruling the database industry nowadays confirms that.

But there was room for improvement in what Clojure provided for defining compoundable data transformations. First of all, the transformations you were writing were not reusable. Indeed, you'd catch yourself writing the same `map` operations over and over again, for instance, had you to do that same operation on different types of collections.

Of course, you could encapsulate these in functions, but that will not avoid the second problem we wanted to highlight: the intermediate `seq` structure generated between the transformation stages. As a matter of fact, each and every step your threading macro passes through yields a new `seq` function, which is not the most efficient possible processing sequence.

Lastly, the transformations you specified were closely tied to the type of input or output they operated on, and that gave the Clojure programming language designers the hassle of redefining all of these operations for any new data abstraction they'd come with while evolving the language.

For all of these reasons, transducers were introduced starting from Clojure 1.7. As the official documentation put it, they are "composable algorithmic transformations. They are independent from the context of their input and output sources and specify only the essence of the transformation in terms of an individual element. ...transducers compose directly, without awareness of input or creation of intermediate aggregates."

In a nutshell, a transducer is a "transformation from one reducing function to another", that is, a means to modify how to handle the way "receiving" the elements of some previous "step" is carried out. For instance, say we define the following transducer (note that transducers are, for the most part, the usual `seq` manipulation functions, but with an arity decremented by one):

```
(map inc)
```

We created a transformation that increments all the elements that some previous stage handed over to this transformation. Let's see an example of that (note the use of `transduce` to apply a transducer on a `seq` function):

```
(transduce (map inc) conj (range 0 3))
```

`(range 0 3)` hands a `seq` function of integers over to the `(map inc)` transducer, which on receiving them, gets them incremented and then, as per the `transduce` function specification, reduces them using the `conj` function.

Transducers are also compoundable. You can achieve this using the traditional `comp` operator, used for traditional function composition, but there's one subtlety you must be aware of. Generally, `comp` is applied left to right, like so:

```
(comp f g ) => f(g(x))
```

In the case of transducers, however, `comp` yields a transformation that looks as if composition was applied from right to left. This is not a change in the way `comp` works, but just how transducers are built. Composing transducers yields a function that changes the inner reducing function, as in the following example:

```
(comp tr1 tr2)=> (fn[] ….. tr2(tr1))
```

So `tr1` is applied on the input before `tr2`, although comp is still applied from left to right!

> To get a deeper understanding of transducer internals and how exactly they happen to be composed from right to left, watch Rich Hickey's talk about the subject at `https://www.youtube.com/watch?v=6mTbuzafcII`.

We are going to use transducers to build a mini-firewall, implementing a two-stage data-transformation, one map and one `filter` stages, and are going to see how this mini-firewall can be interchangeably used on a `vector` or on a `core.async` channel.

How to do it...

1. First of all, be sure to use Clojure 1.7. Here is the Leiningen dependency to include:

    ```
    [org.clojure/clojure "1.7.0-RC1"]
    ```

2. Besides, we are going to use some `core.async` channels in this recipe. Here is the namespace declaration:

    ```
    (ns recipe24.core
      (:require [clojure.java.io :refer :all]
                [clojure.core.async :refer [chan
                                            go
    ```

```
                                         >!
                                         <!
                                         >!!
                                         <!!]])))
```

3. Now, let's define our first transducer, applying a source NAT on the TCP frames that pass through our firewall:

```
(defn source-nat
  [pub-ip
   tcp-frame]
  ;; Change source ip into the public IP Interface
  (assoc tcp-frame :source-ip pub-ip))

(def public-interface "1.2.3.4")
;; This is our public interface IP

(def tr-source-nat (map (partial source-nat
                                 public-interface)))
;; A transducer transforming tcp frames in such a way
;; That Source IP contains the public interface's.
```

4. After that, let's concern ourselves with discarding or accepting TCP frames whose source, destination IPs, and ports are invalidated according to some connection whitelist:

```
(defn accepted?
  [accept-rules
   tcp-frame]
  (not
   (nil?
    (some #{tcp-frame} accept-rules))))
;; Verify if this TCP frame exists within
;; the accept-rules ACL

(def sample-accept-rules [{:source-ip "4.5.3.8" :dest-ip "4.4.3.5"
:dest-port 80}
                          {:source-ip "4.5.3.9" :dest-ip "4.4.3.4"
:dest-port 80}])

(def tr-filter-rules (filter (partial accepted?
                                      sample-accept-rules)))
;; A transducer dropping tcp frames not present
;; in our sample ACL
```

5. Now we build our mini firewall, a transducer resulting from the composition of the previous two transducers. As we'll verify conformity of the connections before proceeding to the source IP NAT on them, we make sure that `tr-filter-rules` comes first in our composition:

```
(def firewall (comp
                tr-filter-rules
                tr-source-nat))
```

6. Let's try our mini-firewall on a vector of TCP frames:

```
(def sample-frames
[{:source-ip "1.1.1.1" :dest-ip "2.3.2.2" :dest-port 10}
 {:source-ip "2.2.2.2" :dest-ip "4.3.4.1" :dest-port 20}
 {:source-ip "4.5.3.8" :dest-ip "4.4.3.5" :dest-port 30}
 {:source-ip "4.5.3.9" :dest-ip "4.4.3.4" :dest-port 80}])

(transduce firewall
           conj
           sample-frames)
;; => [{:source-ip "1.2.3.4", :dest-ip "4.4.3.4", :dest-port 80}]
```

7. And now we'll show how our mini-firewall is reusable. For this, we are going to create a random-TCP frame generator that'll throw some traffic into a `core.async` channel. But this would not be just any channel; it would be one with a transducer, our firewall, attached to it. We'll see what happens when we try to read from it.

 To get a closer look at how to use `core.async`, refer to *Chapter 6, Sharing by Communicating.*

8. First of all, let's write the random TCP frames generator:

```
(def source-hosts [ "4.5.3.8" "4.5.3.9"  "1.1.1.1" "2.2.2.2" ])
(def dest-hosts [ "4.4.3.5" "4.4.3.4"  "2.3.2.2" "4.3.4.1" ])
(def ports [ 80])

(defn get-random-elt
  [v]
    (get v (rand-int (dec (count  v)))))

(defn random-frame []
  {:source-ip (get-random-elt source-hosts)
   :dest-ip (get-random-elt dest-hosts)
   :dest-port (get-random-elt ports)})
```

9. Now it's time to create a `core.async` channel, to which we'll attach the `firewall` transducer. Note that when we attach a transducer to a `core.async` channel, the former must be buffered:

```
(def from-net (chan 10
                          firewall))
```

10. We now need to throw, from time to time, a random TCP frame inside that channel:

```
(defn gen-frames!
  []
  (go
    (while true
      (let [fr (random-frame)]
        (>! from-net fr)
        (Thread/sleep 1000)))))
```

11. We also have to build some function to print the TCP frames that were allowed to pass by the firewall:

```
(defn show-fw-output!
  []
  (while true
    (println "accepted & NAT'ted : "
              (<!! from-net))))
```

12. Let's see what happens when we launch the last two functions:

```
(gen-frames!)
(show-fw-output!)
accepted & NATted :
{:source-ip 1.2.3.4, :dest-ip 4.4.3.4, :dest-port 80}
accepted & NATted :
{:source-ip 1.2.3.4, :dest-ip 4.4.3.5, :dest-port 80}
accepted & NATted :
{:source-ip 1.2.3.4, :dest-ip 4.4.3.5, :dest-port 80}
accepted & NATted :
{:source-ip 1.2.3.4, :dest-ip 4.4.3.5, :dest-port 80}
...
```

13. As you can see, we could only read through the channel "NAT'ted" TCP frames that have been granted access according to `sample-access-rules`. Actually, the transducer attached to the `core.async` channel transforms the data as they are flowing in, and we were able to do that by reusing our transducer specification without having to re-implement it specifically for that particular input type, that is, the channel.

Building a little unification engine with the continuation-passing style

Continuation passing style in functional programming is a paradigm in which the programmer, while building their procedures, specifies a function called the continuation that handles what is to be done after the work of that very procedure is done. While in normal or direct style, return values are often flowing between different callee and caller functions, in continuation passing style the caller just specifies what is to be executed by the callee once it has finished its computation.

In continuation passing style, every function takes an extra argument in relation to its "direct style" counterpart: a continuation that is to be launched on its result. To better understand this, let's consider a simple example. Let's assume you want to use continuation passing style to compute:

```
(* 3 (+ 1 2))
```

To be able to carry this out, you'd want a function that first computes the addition, and then executes a procedure on it:

```
(defn k+
  [a b k]
  (k (+ a b)))
```

You'd also need a function that executes the continuation on the multiplication of two elements:

```
(defn k*
  [a b k ]
  (k (* a b)))
```

And to execute the computation, you'd execute this:

```
(k+ 1 2 #(k* % 3 identity))  ;;=> 9
```

Let's trace the execution of the preceding expression so we grasp how the continuations worked:

1. First, `k+` is called. It computed `1+2`.
2. Then, the continuation is executed with this parameter: `(k* 3 3 identity)`.
3. `3 * 3` is computed.
4. Then, the continuation is executed on the result 9. As this is the last computation, we'll show the result by calling `identity`.

Now one could wonder: what is this style useful for, especially if we consider the fact that it is very likely to be more complicated to follow than direct style? It turns out that continuations are intrinsically used by many compilers in order to optimize their target generations. JavaScript's call-back firing can also be seen as a form of this programming style. Many logic programming engines use this style for their implementation as well. The Scheme programming language even has special support for them through higher-order continuations and its famous `call-cc` function.

As a matter of fact, continuation passing style is an advanced topic. And although it might not be convenient for everyday programming tasks, continuations are extremely useful as higher-order functional tools for compiler designers and logic programming engine builders. Here we will take a closer look at them.

But let's try to answer one question, why aren't continuations as popular in Clojure as in its elder sibling Scheme? We would like to argue that this is tail call optimization's fault. Scheme recognizes recursive calls from the tail position and is able to automatically optimize them, turning them into stack-safe iterative calls. Clojure, as hosted on the JVM, does not provide for this capability in a straight forward manner: In Clojure, you are only able to explicitly emit tail-recursive calls via the `recur` and `trampoline` constructs. Although this empowers you to do efficient recursive and mutual recursive function calling to pass your continuations, it is by no means as convenient as just summoning function names and letting the compiler handle the tail call transformations.

For our next recipe, we'll explore an example implementation of a unification engine written in a continuation passing style. This recipe builds on a scheme implementation, which we adapted to the Clojure recursion constraints (`trampoline`), and which we changed so it yields substitutions instead of unified expressions.

 The scheme implementation we'll base our recipe on is from the book The *Scheme Programming Language* by R. Kent Dybvig, available online at http://www.scheme.com/tspl4/.

But let's explain unification before we show the actual recipe. Unification is about finding which term substitutions may be necessary in order to have equation between two given symbolic expressions. It lies at the heart of many logic programming engines.

 To get a closer look at logic programming, refer to *Chapter 5, Programming with Logic*.

Say, for example, we want to unify the following symbolic expressions:

- `(y (a x t))` and,
- `(y (a (e f) (h j)))`

One solution to this unification problem would be substituting t by (h j) and x by (e f) in the first symbolic expression to arrive at the second one.

The algorithm we are going to use was first described by Robinson in 1965 and is widely used as the basis of many symbolic computation engines. It follows a recursive descent approach and starts by looking simultaneously at the two given symbolic expressions. It advances by one term in both of them at each step. One of two cases can happen:

▶ **We have one symbol at one side, along with a symbolic expression at the other**: We add to the result substitution a mapping of that symbol to that symbolic expression, if the former doesn't occur in the latter; otherwise, we raise a "cycle" error.

▶ **We have two terms that constitute symbolic expressions**: We recursively launch our unification procedure on those two terms, verifying that the first symbols of both of them are the same. Otherwise, we raise a "symbol clash" error.

For a detailed explanation of unification, refer to Unification Theory by Franz Baader and Wayne Snyder, which you can find at http://www.cs.bu.edu/~snyder/publications/UnifChapter.pdf.

Let's now describe our recipe, modeling a simple unification engine between symbolic expressions. We'll use the algorithm we just described, but following continuation passing style.

How to do it...

1. Let's declare the ns of our recipe beforehand. We are going to use zippers, so we'll include this library to be able to summon them:

```
(ns recipe25.core
  (:require [clojure.zip :as z]))
```

2. Using a zipper, we are going to build the occurrence check we are going to use in our unification algorithm:

```
(defn occurs?
  [s t]
  (if (seq? t)  ;; If second term is a seq
    (let [zpr  (z/zipper seq? identity conj t)]
      ;; We create a zipper to walk it
      (loop [loc (-> zpr z/down)]
```

```
;; We begin at the first element of the zipper
  (if (-> loc z/end?)
    false
;; We reached the end, yet we were not able
;; to find the first term. It does not occur
    (if (= s (-> loc z/node))
        true
;; One node of our zipper happens to be equal
;; to the first term. We immediately return true
        (recur (-> loc z/next))))))))
;; else we recur over the next zipper element
  (= s t)))
;; If t is not a seq, we say that s occurs in t if they are equal
```

3. The substitutions result of our unification program will be a map, in which keys are the terms that will be substituted by their respective values. As we'll use recursive calls, it will difficult for us to pass along the substitution map through `recur` constructs, so we'll set it as a global atom for the sake of simplicity:

```
(def s (atom {}))
```

4. At every step of the algorithm, we'll need to apply the substitutions we managed to symbols that cross our path so that we are sure we end up with exactly one substitution per term. For this, we'll build a function that trades a term for its related replacement, according to the current value of the substitution atom, and systematically apply it before trying to find any new substitutions. Here is the substitution application function:

```
(defn apply-subst
  [u]
  (if (seq? u); If u is a seq
    (replace @s u)
    ;; We apply the value referred by the s atom
    ;; as a substitution map so to respectively
    ;; replace u terms by their counterparts
    ;; in s
    (if-let [subst  (get @s u)] ;; Else, u is a scalar
      subst ;; If u occurs in s we return its counterpart
      u))) ;; else we leave it as is.
```

5. Now we'll concern ourselves with the design of the unification algorithm. We'll first need a utility function that'll try to find if there is a substitution that can be applied to the current terms from the first and second symbolic expressions. This function will check for the "cycles", that is, it will raise an error if the term we are checking for substitution occurs in its potential substitute. Note that we are using continuation passing style as we are not returning values but executing success or failure functions, respectively labeled `ks` and `kf`. Note also that we are not executing functions but returning them instead, so we can pass them through `trampoline`, and efficiently handle the mutual tail-recursive calls of our algorithm. `uni`, the main function for unifying expressions, will be implemented later. As we need it at this stage, we need to declare it:

```
(declare uni) ;; uni declaration

(defn try-subst
  [u v ks kf]
  (let [u (apply-subst u)]
;; First, we exchange u for any known
;; substitute, so we don't unify the same
;; thing with two different terms
    (if (not (symbol? u))
;; This is not a symbol, it is an expression
      #(uni u v ks kf)
;; Launch uni, the "main" expressions unifier
      (let [v (apply-subst v )]
;; Same logic for right hand expression term
        (cond
          (= u v) #(ks @s)
;; The terms are equal, nothing to do, we
;; run the success function over the same content of s
          (occurs? u v) #(kf "Error : Cycle!")
;; Occur Check error
          :default #(ks (swap! s
                              assoc
                              u
                              v )))))))
;; Else, We found a new substitution
;; to be added to our substitutions atom s
```

6. The `main` unifier function, which is able to recursively unify symbolic expressions, is then implemented. Note how the case where we need to unify two sub-expressions made us declare an inner function and `trampoline` it in order to recursively iterate the process of unification over the elements of these two sub-expressions. We had a success function set to a recursive call to that same inner function:

```
(defn uni
  [u v ks kf]
  (cond
    (symbol? u) #(try-subst u v  ks kf)
;; Try to find substitutions if the left hand
;; term is a symbol
    (symbol? v) #(try-subst v u  ks kf)
;; Else, try it for the right hand term
;; If we have two symbolic expressions with no name clash,
;; we unify all of their inner terms, one by one, using
;; a recursion. We'll use this inner function for this.
    (and (= (first u) (first v))
         (= (count u) (count v))) (letfn [(internal-symbols
                                           [u v]
                                           (if (nil? u)
                                             #(ks @s)
;; End of the recursion, run success on the value referred by s
                                             (fn[]
;; else, recurse over uni
                                               (uni (first u)
                                                    (first v)
                                                    (fn[_]
                                                      (internal-symbols (next u)
                                                                        (next v)))
;; With a success function making us recurse over the next terms
                                                    kf))))]
;; and the failure function

;; For symbolic expressions, trampoline this inner function
;; so to initiate a recursive walk of every one of their
;; children expressions.
                                    (trampoline internal-symbols (next u)
                                                                 (next v)))
;; else we had a symbol clash!
    :default (kf "Error : Symbol Clash!")))
```

7. Finally, we'll have to define our `unify` function, which instantiates the proper continuations for the `uni` function we just built. We'll use `identity` as success and failure continuations so as to show the substitution after the end of all the computations or simply spit any of the errors we may happen to encounter. One interesting property of continuation passing style is that we can change the behavior of our engine. We could have set the success continuation to some procedure that applies the result substitution to the terms that would have caused our program to output two identical terms at the very end. This would show that the unification worked. Once again, it is a trampolined call as we are making use of tail mutual recursion. Here is the implementation of unify:

```
(defn unify
  [u v]
  (let [_  (reset! s {})]
    (trampoline uni
                u
                v
                identity
                identity)))
```

8. Et voilà! Let's see how little unifier performs. First of all, let's check for a valid unification problem. Emit the following at your REPL:

```
(unify '(y (a x t)) '( y (a (e f) (h j))))
```

9. You'll get this result:

```
;; => {t (h j), x (e f)}
```

10. Now let's generate a symbol clash. Ask for two terms to be unified as follows:

```
(unify '(a (x y z)) '(b (x y z)))
```

11. You'll get this result:

```
;; => "Error : Symbol Clash!"
```

12. Finally, let's see how the unifier reacts in the face of a cyclic problem statement. Try this unification of two expressions:

```
(unify '(y x z) '(y (x t) z) )
```

13. The output is as follows:

```
"Error : Cycle!"
```

Index

Thank you for buying
Clojure Data Structures and Algorithms Cookbook

About Packt Publishing

Packt, pronounced 'packed', published its first book, *Mastering phpMyAdmin for Effective MySQL Management*, in April 2004, and subsequently continued to specialize in publishing highly focused books on specific technologies and solutions.

Our books and publications share the experiences of your fellow IT professionals in adapting and customizing today's systems, applications, and frameworks. Our solution-based books give you the knowledge and power to customize the software and technologies you're using to get the job done. Packt books are more specific and less general than the IT books you have seen in the past. Our unique business model allows us to bring you more focused information, giving you more of what you need to know, and less of what you don't.

Packt is a modern yet unique publishing company that focuses on producing quality, cutting-edge books for communities of developers, administrators, and newbies alike. For more information, please visit our website at www.packtpub.com.

About Packt Open Source

In 2010, Packt launched two new brands, Packt Open Source and Packt Enterprise, in order to continue its focus on specialization. This book is part of the Packt open source brand, home to books published on software built around open source licenses, and offering information to anybody from advanced developers to budding web designers. The Open Source brand also runs Packt's open source Royalty Scheme, by which Packt gives a royalty to each open source project about whose software a book is sold.

Writing for Packt

We welcome all inquiries from people who are interested in authoring. Book proposals should be sent to author@packtpub.com. If your book idea is still at an early stage and you would like to discuss it first before writing a formal book proposal, then please contact us; one of our commissioning editors will get in touch with you.

We're not just looking for published authors; if you have strong technical skills but no writing experience, our experienced editors can help you develop a writing career, or simply get some additional reward for your expertise.

Mastering Clojure Data Analysis

Leverage the power and flexibility of Clojure through this practical guide to data analysis

Eric Rochester   PACKT open source*

Mastering Clojure Data Analysis

ISBN: 978-1-78328-413-9   Paperback: 340 pages

Leverage the power and flexibility of Clojure through this practical guide to data analysis

1. Explore the concept of data analysis using established scientific methods combined with the powerful Clojure language.

2. Master Naïve Bayesian Classification, Benford's Law, and much more in Clojure.

3. Learn with the help of examples drawn from exciting, real-world data.

Clojure High Performance Programming

Understand performance aspects and write high performance code with Clojure

Shantanu Kumar   PACKT open source*

Clojure High Performance Programming

ISBN: 978-1-78216-560-6   Paperback: 152 pages

Understand performance aspects and write high performance code with Clojure

1. See how the hardware and the JVM impact performance.

2. Learn which Java features to use with Clojure, and how.

3. Deep dive into Clojure's concurrency and state primitives.

4. Discover how to design Clojure programs for performance.

Please check **www.PacktPub.com** for information on our titles

Clojure Reactive Programming

ISBN: 978-1-78398-666-8   Paperback: 232 pages

Design and implement highly reusable reactive applications by integrating different frameworks with Clojure

1. Learn how to leverage the features of functional reactive programming using Clojure.

2. Create dataflow-based systems that are the building blocks of reactive programming.

3. Learn different Functional Reactive Programming frameworks and techniques by implementing real-world examples.

Clojure for Machine Learning

ISBN: 978-1-78328-435-1   Paperback: 292 pages

Successfully leverage advanced machine learning techniques using the Clojure ecosystem

1. Covers a lot of machine learning techniques with Clojure programming.

2. Encompasses precise patterns in data to predict future outcomes using various machine learning techniques.

3. Packed with several machine learning libraries available in the Clojure ecosystem.

Please check **www.PacktPub.com** for information on our titles

www.ingramcontent.com/pod-product-compliance
Lightning Source LLC
Chambersburg PA
CBHW060556060326
40690CB00017B/3724